THE LIBERTIES OF WIT

Humanism, Criticism, and the Civic Mind

By the Same Author:

Problems in American Government (1952, 1957)

The Regulation of Businessmen (1954)

Political Life: Why People Get Involved in Politics (1959)

THE LIBERTIES OF WIT

Humanism, Criticism, and the Civic Mind

by ROBERT E. LANE

New Haven and London: Yale University Press, 1961

Copyright © 1961 by Yale University.
Set in Linotype Baskerville type and
printed in the United States of America by
The Carl Purington Rollins Printing-Office of
the Yale University Press, New Haven, Connecticut.
All rights reserved. This book may not be
reproduced, in whole or in part, in any form
(except by reviewers for the public press),
without written permission from the publishers.

Library of Congress catalog card number: 61–14434

Acknowledgments

IT was the invitation to give the Falk Lectures at the Carnegie Institute of Technology in February 1960 that provided the occasion and, somehow, the courage to open up a subject which had long been weighing on my mind. For the opportunity to give these lectures (then entitled "Through a Glass, Darkly"), and for the helpful comments I received there from the critical but tolerant audience, I am most grateful. From the Fellows of Branford College I have received bibliographical and other help which has reduced my rate of error and increased my understanding of a difficult and vital field of learning. In a special sense I am indebted to Monroe Beardsley, who must in no way bear the burden of responsibility for what I have said here (indeed, he has many reservations) but whose patient and generous review of an earlier draft helped me to frame more carefully and precisely ideas which then were loosely and sometimes misleadingly stated. To Henry Brosin, Ruth Deutsch, David Easton, Barbara and Fred Greenstein, Helen Lane, and Robert Wilson, I am grateful for the time they took to hear the lectures or to read the manuscript, penetrate its obscurities, and show me how to make my story clearer. Charles Blitzer kindly led me to the present title. Finally, my thanks are due to the Ford Foundation for assistance with publication.

R. E. L.

New Haven
March 1961

To I. J. S. and I. S. S.

Contents

But we, brave Britons, foreign laws despised,
And kept unconquered, and uncivilized;
Fierce for the liberties of wit, and bold,
We still defied the Romans, as of old.
.   .   .   .

Fear not the anger of the wise to raise
Those best can bear reproof, who merit praise.

—ALEXANDER POPE, *Essay on Criticism*

1. Introduction: Humanism, Criticism, and Citizenship

I T has been a long time since anyone took seriously the question of whether the study of poetry, or at least certain kinds of poetry, is detrimental to the development of civic virtue. To the modern ear it seems to be a foolish question, although the spirit behind it has certainly been heard in the recent investigations on the effects of comic books and television on the young. But it is not a foolish question, nor was Plato's answer a foolish one, however wrong it may seem to us now. He argued, as is well known, that poetry that did not uphold his views of justice, or that implied that the unjust might be happier than the just or that they could avoid the consequences of their injustice by appealing to the Gods, or that portrayed the Gods as indulging in violence or other evil practices, should be banned. He opposed dialogue in poetry because it required impersonation and this led to evil consequences. Poetry that emphasized "the image of the good" and that developed the heroic qualities and courage of men was to remain and to serve important purposes in the training of guardians of the society. He said:

> Let our artists rather be those who are gifted to discern the true nature of the beautiful and graceful; then will our youth dwell in a land of health, amid fair sights and sounds, and receive the good in everything; and beauty,

the effluence of fair works, shall flow into the eye and
ear, like a health-giving breeze from a purer region, and
insensibly draw the soul from earliest years into likeness
and sympathy with the beauty of reason.[1]

How do we "draw the soul from earliest years into likeness
and sympathy with the beauty of reason"? That is our problem. Like Plato, I am concerned with the citizen and, in a
sense, with the "guardian," for most of what I have to say
refers to college education and therefore to the education of
those who will be guardians in one way or another. My concern is with the way in which the humanities and the social
sciences together prepare men for an adult life in which they
must bear some responsibility for themselves and for others
as well. Like Plato, too, I am concerned with how education
shapes the mind so that it may "discern the true nature" of
things. And, finally, also like Plato, I run a risk.[2] I run the
risk of tampering with the creative spirit whose conditions
of survival and growth are, in fact, the conditions of our own
growth and maturity. Have I moved with booted feet into a
garden of jasmine and lillies? I hope this is not in any way the
case. God help me if in some oblique and minor manner it
should turn out that way.

My argument is a simple one; it has two prongs. I shall be
saying, in the first place, that there are certain ways of thinking that we use in our teaching and writing, certain approaches
to knowledge, certain styles of investigation, which, hallowed
though they may be by centuries of use, fail to advance the
inquiries of which they are a part, and I shall try to show why

---

1. *The Republic,* Jowett translation (London, 1927 ed.), Book III, p. 401.
2. With more poetic imagination than history, Henry Murray, the father of
the TAT tests, puts it this way: "When Plato, envious of Homer's enormous
influence in Greece, banished poets and myth-makers from his Republic, he
deprived it of the springs of charismatic power, and so, when it came to a
showdown with the masses, his beautifully reasoned books were plowed under
by the passionate myths of the poet-authors of the Bible." ("A Mythology for
Grownups," *The Saturday Review,* Jan. 23, 1960, p. 11.)

this is the case.[3] In the second place, I will argue that many
of these ways of thinking learned in school tend systematically
to undercut the citizen's capacity to grapple with and understand the political and social world which challenges him on
every hand.

Where are these defective ways of thinking located? They
are everywhere, but not everywhere in the same abundance
and not everywhere do they persist in the same state of unconscious felicity, unruffled by the clarifying winds of modern
times. I am a political scientist, a social scientist, a behavioral
scientist, but I take the liberty here to search on the other side
of that chasm which has opened between the humanities and
the social sciences for such evidence of these troublesome difficulties as I have found to exist where I am at home, in the
materials of politics. It is a liberty under any circumstances,
but perhaps more so where the departmentalization of knowledge transcends the principle of the specialization of labor, as
is often true on the American campus. It is a justified liberty
only if the spirit that prompts it is humble and the language
that carries the message says, among other things, "welcome,
all, to a common inquiry."

In the house of the humanities there are many mansions.
How different are the ways of thinking of the literary critic,
the historian, the symbolic logician! Perhaps the phrase "liberal arts" more nearly describes the general area of concern
in this analysis. Is there something central here? I have heard
philosophers and historians each claim that among these arts
his discipline is central. Northrop Frye "finds that literature
is the central division of the humanities, flanked on one side
by history and on the other by philosophy."[4] Perhaps the
question has only a vague reference and is better set aside. In
any event I have selected a focus that lies within the humanistic tradition. I have chosen literary criticism as an area where

---

3. For an earlier and more general discussion of this issue, see Max Eastman,
The Literary Mind: Its Place in an Age of Science (New York, Scribner, 1935).
4. *Anatomy of Criticism* (Princeton University Press, 1957), p. 12.

the points I wish to make can find illustration. I have picked
a place where there is today outstanding strength; if my thesis
should prove convincing here it would be more convincing
elsewhere. This is a discussion, then, on the ways of thinking,
the methods of analysis, employed in literary criticism. But
this is only an illustration; to the extent that these analytical
modes find currency in the other humanistic disciplines and
in the social sciences as well, the points made have a wider
application.

On one item there will be misunderstanding: I speak not
of the reading of literature, not of the enjoyment of poetry,
not of that total participation in the dramatic act which comes
to the sensitive audience. These experiences are, so to speak,
the rewards for living. I speak in these pages only of the
modes of analyzing literature, the ways of thinking employed
to explain how a poem achieves its effect, or, more broadly,
the theory of literature. So now let us begin.

What do we want of the citizen? Aristotle and Bryce think
of the answer in terms of his political functions, Bryce as a
member of the democratic public, Aristotle as a man eligible
for governmental office and jury duty.[5] Both are concerned
with his skills and his moral qualities. Most nations have codes
of behavior and attitudes that are essential for decent citizenship. C. E. Merriam, in a study of nine of them, finds that
these codes usually include obedience to law, loyalty to and
respect for the regime and its ideology, a certain amount of
self-control, a willingness to sacrifice for the community, and
sometimes a sense of the mission or destiny of a people.[6] But
one might also focus upon how a citizen solves the conflicts
between his private needs and his public duties. Thus, as H.
M. Roelofs suggests, a citizen must at the same time be loyal
and yet independently critical; he must support the authorities

5. James Bryce, *Promoting Good Citizenship* (Boston, Houghton Mifflin,
1913); Aristotle, *Politics*, Ellis translation (London, 1912), especially chs. V–XIII.
6. *The Making of Citizens* (Chicago University Press, 1931).

but be ready to defy them; he must sacrifice for the common good but protect himself against exploitation.[7]

We want all of these things of our citizens and more. We want them to have democratic values and the personality structure to sustain these effectively. We want them to have the skills to take part in civic or social life. We want them to understand their heritage. We want them to be informed on public affairs. And we want them to have mental clarity, the mental habits and equipment to cope adequately with the public questions with which they are confronted. Here is our second focus: the mental clarity of the citizen, the "sound mind" that comes to terms with life, seeks to understand it, and, understanding, deals with it.

Mental clarity could mean anything from a platform on which to say "I disagree with you" to a concept of complete order and rationality—as in the Mind of God. I mean, and will deal with, the following things: First, I mean an understanding of the philosophical foundation on which an inquiry is premised and an awareness of the consequences of this foundation for the type of questions asked. Second, I mean an awareness and analysis of the theoretical propositions that underlie statements of fact, historical accounts of events, evaluations of poetry or politics, and casual comments on the events of the day. (For example, knowing that the statement, "President Kennedy is doing a good job," involves an implicit theory of the presidency and of current domestic and international affairs.) Third, I mean, by mental clarity, a sophistication about the way concepts are formed and the uses of the classificatory systems we inevitably use in every statement. Very close to this, in the fourth place, I mean a knowledge of the relation between language and the real world. I mean, fifth, an idea of how propositions about reality may be tested, a firm grasp on the more reliable methods of verification either actually available or useful as a way of thinking about "truth."

7. *The Tension of Citizenship, Private Man and Public Duty* (New York, Rinehart, 1957).

Sixth, mental clarity, as I use it, means a knowledge of the processes of evaluation and judging and employment of these processes when evaluation is required. Seventh, I mean a capacity to differentiate between fantasying and directed thinking—an awareness and control over thought processes. Finally, I mean the organization of experience so as to give a general clarity to life which might embrace the emotional, the moral, and the purposive, as well as the purely instrumental clarity we have been considering. I cannot imagine any field of learning, particularly not my own, *establishing* clarity of this kind. In what sense does the example set by the study of literature contribute to it?

This is not the way the question is usually put. The effect of literary study on citizenship and character in general has, for a variety of reasons, been discussed in terms of morality, character, loyalty, taste, even politics, and other features of human nature which are important and which bear upon our later discussion of "the organization of experience." Many voices are raised to advance the cause of literature in these respects; and very few are so restrictive as Plato—perhaps Tolstoy is the most important of these. A sampling of these arguments would show Shelley arguing for poetry as an influence on morality more important than that of religion, and Arnold arguing that poetry is or is about to be a substitute for religion. Van Wyck Brooks argued for a critical study of literature in the United States as a means of raising the standards of taste of a backward nation;[8] I. A. Richards argued for criticism as a means of refining taste everywhere.[9] Irving Babbitt argued that the real school for character and imagination is the study of great literature, and no doubt this is generally accepted by many critics today.[10] It is reflected in the Great Books doctrine

8. "The Critics and Young America" (1917) in Irving Babbitt and others, *Criticism in America, Its Function and Status* (New York, Harcourt, Brace, 1924), pp. 116–51.

9. *Principles of Literary Criticism* (London, Kegan Paul, Trench, Trubner, 1925), pp. 32, 33, 57.

10. *Literature and the American College* (Boston, Houghton Mifflin, 1908).

of St. John's and other schools. There are those, like J. Douglas
Bush, who argue that literary study will serve to offset the
mechanization and inhumanity of life,[11] and in a similar vein
Kenneth Burke argues for a stress in a utilitarian age upon
aesthetic values. But, for Burke, literature has a balancing
function: in an aesthetic age, literature should stress utilitarian values.[12] W. E. Hocking argues that art is necessary for
"the heavy task of world-unifying," and hence that literature
can serve national purposes in a time of conflict.[13] Literature
and art are often said to bind a people together. And because,
on the individual level, the level of the lonely reader, literature restores the soul and gives a sense of purpose, its social
function as an agent of mental therapy may be argued with
some cogency.[14]

The relationship of the study of literature to politics is of
special interest to me. That literature has a political effect
seems agreed upon; the attitude of the writer toward this
effect is a matter of controversy. On one side of this argument,
the "responsibility" side, if I may use the term that is often
employed, are, among others, Archibald MacLeish, W. H.
Auden, Van Wyck Brooks, and Jean-Paul Sartre. On the other
side, along with Oscar Wilde, are Allen Tate, his teacher, John
Crowe Ransom, and T. S. Eliot. Sartre, writing in 1945, says:

> I hold Flaubert and Goncourt responsible for the repres-
> sion which followed the Commune, because they wrote
> not a single line to prevent them. It may be said that it
> was none of their business: but was the case of Calas the
> business of Voltaire? the sentence on Dreyfus the business

11. "The Real Maladjustment," Harvard Foundation for Advanced Study
and Research *Newsletter,* September 30, 1959.

12. "The Status of Art" and "Program" in *Counter-Statement* (Chicago University Press, Phoenix Books, 1957; first edition, 1931).

13. *Strength of Men and Nations, A Message to the USA vis-a-vis the USSR*
(New York, Harper, 1959), p. 28.

14. See Monroe C. Beardsley, *Aesthetics, Problems in the Philosophy of
Criticism* (New York, Harcourt, Brace, 1958), p. 575.

of Zola? the administration of the Congo the business of
Gide? Each one of these writers in some particular circumstances of his life, weighed up his responsibility as a
writer. The occupation taught us ours. Since by our existence we influence our time, we must decide that this influence shall be deliberate.[15]

And Allen Tate, that brilliantly exasperating commentator
on literature *and* politics, argues that the poet loses sight of
his main responsibility when he deals with social or political
issues:

> To suggest that poets tell men in crisis what to do, to
> insist that *as poets* they acknowledge themselves as legis-
> lators of the social order, is to ask them to shirk their
> specific responsibility, which is quite simply the reality of
> man's experience, not what his experience ought to be,
> in any age.[16]

The differences in the concreteness of language and ability to
communicate exactly what is meant (in spite of the fact that
Sartre's is a translation) apparent in these two passages are
not fortuitous; they are, I think, quite generally associated
with the respective political views of Sartre and Tate. I am
still not clear on the way Tate thinks a poet should relate to
what he calls "the reality of man's experience" and what he
should do about it. It might be observed that Sartre, too, in
his way, is quite simply appealing for a close inspection of
certain portions of "the reality of man's experience."

A writer or critic need not, of course, display his political
badge openly; indeed, the better the writer the more the political implications of what he says will be an integral and only
partially revealed feature of his work. In a subtle way William
Empson shows how this may be done as he examines the way

15. "The Case for Responsible Literature," *Partisan Review, 12* (1945), 307.
16. Allen Tate, *The Man of Letters in the Modern World* (New York, Meridian Books, 1955), p. 32.

in which ironical humor, pastoral themes, and the class status of character roles in much literature convey conservative ideas to the reader.[17] Part of the effect of literature and literary study upon the citizen then is a political effect.

But for all this discussion, thought, and argument, I must agree with Allen Tate: "The relation of poetry and of other high imaginative literature to social action was not sufficiently considered in the attacks and counter attacks of the past ten years. No one knows precisely what the relation is."[18] No more do we know what the influence of literature and literary study may be on the taste, morality, character, ideology, and politics of the time. It seems that we know more about the public impact of radio, television, and the cinema, and that is little enough. We know more about the effect of one Kate Smith broadcast series than we do about the effect of a term study of *Paradise Lost*. Our task would be somewhat easier if there were more empirical evidence at hand; but since the question about mental clarity and the humanities has never been put, we are left in our particular realm of inquiry, unfortunately, all too free. We shall return to these matters; in the meantime we must focus upon the readers' guide, the literary critic.

I don't suppose there ever was a time when students in school read the literature considered great in their society without the assistance of some teacher or scholar to help them understand it. But if there was, that time is now long past, and the specialization and scholarship which today contribute to such an understanding have now become formidable in the extreme. The field of learning so developed includes literary theory, literary criticism, literary history, or in older terminology, philology. The theoretical aspects border on and include parts of aesthetics; the literary history is cognate with general history; literary criticism has an applied aspect in book reviewing; and philology, a vague term which René

18. *Man of Letters*, p. 31.
17. *Some Versions of Pastoral* (London, Chatto & Windus, 1950).

Wellek and Austin Warren suggest might better be abandoned,[19] bears some historical relation to linguistics and semantics. Although these elements of the study of literature "interpenetrate" each other, our primary concern is with the theory and practice of literary criticism, which we take to be the non-historical parts of the scope and method of the study of literature. Our concern, then, is with the methods of thought, the ways of thinking encouraged in this study, not the ways of thinking of the poets and writers who themselves create the literature.

The critic's role (I will use the term "critic" to cover both critic and theorist) is a difficult, demanding, and important one. In its simplest terms it is, as we have said, to help the reader. Eliot says this is done in two ways, "by the elucidation of works of art and the correction of taste."[20] Auden suggests that the critic is to do this by teaching him "how to see the relevance to his own experience of works of art" dealing with contemporary and historical materials strange to him.[21] Richards emphasizes the "endeavor to discriminate between experiences and to evaluate them"[22] as the means to the same end. In these personal terms, most critics would agree that their function is to facilitate those ennobling, enriching, and organizing effects which often follow from the proper reading of poetry, drama, and fiction.

It is a natural expansion of this ambition to think of the mission of criticism as a guardianship of taste for a society, a stewardship in the field of the arts. Allen Tate emphasizes this. "His literary responsibility," he says of the modern man of letters (both critics and authors), "is thus what it always has been—the recreation and application of literary standards,

19. *Theory of Literature* (New York, Harcourt, Brace, Harvest Books, 1956), p. 27.

20. "The Function of Criticism," reprinted in Irving Howe, ed., *Modern Literary Criticism* (Boston, Beacon Press, 1958), p. 39.

21. W. H. Auden, "Criticism in a Mass Society," in Donald A. Stauffer, ed., *The Intent of the Critic* (Princeton University Press, 1941), p. 133.

22. *Principles of Literary Criticism*, p. 2.

which, in order to be effectively literary, must be more than
literary. His task is to preserve the integrity, the purity, and
the reality of language wherever and for whatever purpose it
may be used."[23] His reference to "more than literary" is to a
body of religious thought and humanistic goals which are, at
least in the writing I have seen, only suggested. Like Tate,
Auden sees the critic as the guardian of taste, as, indeed, do
the great historical figures of criticism, Aristotle, Coleridge,
Shelley, Arnold. But Auden argues further that this should
be in the interest of literary democracy, a sharing of power:
"If we are ever to achieve a democratic culture," he says, "we
must all begin by admitting the fact of this dictatorship [of
taste] and the critics themselves must accept responsibility
and not mislead the public."[24] In order to do this each critic
must first state clearly the values which inform his judgments,
and secondly must seek "to persuade others to do without
him, to realize that the gifts of the spirit are never to be at
second hand."[25] In this he echoes Edmund Burke's dictum:
"Every man his own critic."

Looking in the other direction, toward the creative writers
who produce the material thus criticized, there is, I think, a
certain ambivalence on the part of the critical fraternity. On
the one hand they do not pretend to tell writers how to create;
they shun the notion of how-to-do-it books; they do not pub-
lish books on rhetoric and style. Indeed, based on their concepts of the autonomy of art and the individuality of artistic
production they may even worry lest they inadvertently have
such an influence as I. A. Richards did after his experiments
with "Practical Criticism." "I am not without fears," he says,
"that my efforts may prove of assistance to young poets (and
others) desiring to increase their sales."[26] On the other hand,

23. *Man of Letters,* p. 20.
24. Auden, "Criticism in a Mass Society," p. 141.
25. Auden, p. 146.
26. I. A. Richards, *Practical Criticism* (New York, Harcourt, Brace, 1954),
fn. p. 9.

by establishing canons of taste and judgment and by discussing
the means whereby they conceive artistic effects to be produced, they must inevitably affect the sensibility (a magic
word) of the artist. "The critical activity," says T. S. Eliot,
"finds its highest, its true fulfillment in a kind of union with
creation in the labour of the artist."[27]

An outsider, I think, is bound to consider the relations of
the theory of literature as expounded by the critics to the
writing of literature as at least interesting, and possibly as a
focal point of special difficulties. Generally speaking, both
the behavioral scientist and the natural scientist develop
theories in order to understand phenomena, and seek to understand phenomena in order to control them. This provides
a genuine incentive to develop theories which are comprehensive, public (not based upon incommunicable private experiences), and testable. The reluctance of the literary critic
to influence the writer, and the reticence of articulate men to
talk about this aspect of their work creates an ambiguous
relationship between theory and practice that poses a problem
for both creation and criticism.

In carrying out his mission—which we have said is to develop the sensibilities of his readers and, for some, to guard
the standards of culture in a society—the critic must in the
first place define the field of objects which he seeks to appraise
and analyze. What is art or what is an aesthetic object? What
is literature? What is poetry? Then, there are questions dealing with the ways of describing such objects: the rhythm,
sound, language, structure, form, ideas, characters, themes,
and so forth. There is the problem of interpretation, of which
an important part is the explication of meaning. Richards
identifies four kinds: sense, feeling, tone, intention.[28] A more
useful analysis of the kinds of meaning is suggested by Beardsley, where he first identifies the cognitive and emotive import
of a work, and then suggests a tripartite division of what in-

27. "The Function of Criticism," p. 44.
28. *Practical Criticism*, pp. 179–88.

formation the cognitive import (or purport) offers: information about the beliefs of the speaker, information about his
feelings, and information about some of his other characteristics.[29] The critic asks how the author achieves his effects
(point of view, irony, metaphor, symbolism, ambiguity, and
so forth). And finally he must work out for himself some
theory of evaluation or borrow somebody else's.

In order to do this he must know a very great deal, indeed,
even if he restricts himself to the central task of the critic:
the interpretation and explanation of the nature and effects
of a work (and not its creation).[30] As the new critics point out
with such eloquent insistence, the critic must know the work
he is analyzing; he must, moreover, know it in the body of
work of which it is a part, because comparison is an essential
mode of analysis and helps in explaining the sense of the
analytical findings. He must know history, as Wellek and
Warren point out, else how would he know the difference
between an original work and a derivative or imitative one.
One might argue, as Monroe Beardsley does, that the critic
qua critic who confines himself to the properties of the work
and to its effects upon an audience must, on logical grounds,
find originality an irrelevant criterion of evaluation. This is a
valuable distinction and if applied should help to raise the
standards of criticism. Unfortunately there is very substantial
evidence to show that in practice almost all judgments are
affected by associative thinking, halo effects, stimulus generalization, and other "contaminating" influences.[31]

The critic must know language, not just in the etymological
sense, although this may be useful as Kenneth Burke often
shows, but because so much of the force of a work depends
upon the many meanings of a word, its previous usage and connotative implications, he must know how language has been
employed in the widest range of works. Although his view may

29. Beardsley, *Aesthetics*, pp. 116–19.
30. See below, pp. 30–31.
31. See Beardsley, pp. 460, 490–91.

represent a minority opinion, Stanley Hyman defines modern criticism as "the organized use of non-literary techniques and bodies of knowledge to obtain insights into literature."[32] Chief among these are the social sciences, particularly anthropology, psychology, psychiatry, and sociology; and with this chrestomathy before him the critic must somehow learn their languages and concepts, or a few of them anyway, to get the "leverage" that these extrinsic disciplines are now in a position to give. And in addition to all this knowledge, he must have a special sensitivity, a gift for penetrating the forms of language and perceiving meanings which are subliminal to the ordinary eye.

The product of these inquiries is a body of knowledge and an applied literature that is bound to impress the outsider with its grace and penetrating insight, its imagination and capacity to give delight. Increasingly it is becoming organized and the belle-lettristic quality going the way of amateurism everywhere. As Wellek and Warren point out, the student of literature "must translate his experience of literature into intellectual terms, assimilate it to a coherent scheme which must be rational if it is to be knowledge."[33] This sounds, indeed, like that branch of knowledge which is called science, and, although I think most critics will disagree with him, Frye dismisses the opposition to this view as "absurd." He says "It seems absurd to say that there *may* be a scientific element in criticism where there are dozens of learned journals based on the assumption that there is, and hundreds of scholars engaged in scientific procedures related to literary criticism. . . . Either literary criticism is scientific, or all of these highly trained and intelligent scholars are wasting their time on some kind of pseudo-science like phrenology."[34] He is not alone. Hyman says that "increasingly we can expect it [literary criti-

32. *The Armed Vision* (abridged edition, New York, Knopf, Vintage Books, 1955), p. 3.
33. *Theory of Literature*, p. 3.
34. *Anatomy of Criticism*, p. 8.

cism] to move in a scientific direction; that is, toward a formal methodology and system of procedures that can be objectively transmitted."[35] Such a prospect causes a shudder to run through the frames of most literary critics, and they go to some pains to deny this, indeed to deny that science and literary criticism have anything whatsoever in common. Ransom, for example, is adamant on this point; poetic materials, he says, "are such as to fall outside the possible range of science."[36] Perhaps our comments will contribute to an understanding of this issue—and perhaps to the shudder as well.

I have devoted a little time to an outline of the field of literary criticism—and, of course, I have not portrayed it in anything like its rich and magnificent florescence—in order to give a background to the discussion of the manner in which the study of literature *guided in this way* contributes to the development of democratic citizenship. My chief concern is with the ways of thinking that it instills and encourages; my chief ambition is to seek a solution to the problems that this presents; and my chief method is to examine the presuppositions and the methods of literary criticism in some detail.

35. *The Armed Vision*, p. 11.
36. John Crowe Ransom, *The New Criticism* (Norfolk, Conn., New Directions, 1941), p. xi.

2. Original Error

I will argue in the following chapters that our common tasks of training and discovery (common, that is, to the humanities and the social sciences) are impeded by frequent misunderstanding of the nature of theory, a failure to apply what is already known about the uses and the abuses of typing and classifying our materials, ignorance of procedures for verifying our hypotheses, a reluctance to employ the available tools of empirical research for the purpose, and carelessness in patrolling our language so that we are not deceived by the words we use. But as I speculate about the persistence of these wayward tendencies, I am increasingly led to believe that there is, at the bottom of things, some original error which increases our tendencies to ask the wrong questions and set off in the wrong direction. In any inquiry, that of the citizen, the scientist, or the critic, the first problem and often the most difficult one is the framing of the question to be asked. This initial step "is like a ship leaving port for a distant destination," says F.S.C. Northrop. "A very slight erroneous deviation in taking one's bearings at the beginning may result in entirely missing one's mark at the end, regardless of the sturdiness of one's craft or the excellence of one's subsequent seamanship."[1] But if he consistently takes the wrong bearings, probably a man's compass is at fault.

1. *The Logic of the Sciences and the Humanities* (New York, Meridian Books, 1959), p. 1.

If I have correctly diagnosed this original error in literary criticism, it lies in the metaphysical foundation of the critic's world. Everyone is familiar with the general contours of what is broadly speaking an idealist-nominalist, absolutist-relativist controversy in the field of aesthetics. The complex of ideas associated with the idealist position include, in addition to absolutism, the notions of universality and "the intrinsic." The particular idealism we have in mind is Platonic, rather than Berkeleyan, which, if I understand it correctly, has different consequences for aesthetic theory. It is grounded in a philosophical tradition of great weight, and greatly reinforced by Kant's *Critique of Judgment*. Wordsworth's concept of a "permanent style" and Coleridge's universal forms seem to be reflections of this philosophic position. It has its modern adherents.

In discussing the way in which he has dealt with particular poems in *The Well Wrought Urn*, Cleanth Brooks refers to "the general criteria against which the poems may be measured." He goes on to say, "If there is any absolutism implied, I prefer not to conceal it, but to bring it out in the open."[2] John Crowe Ransom, in criticizing Richards, states that "He very nearly severed the dependence of poetic effect upon any objective knowledge or belief."[3] The context implies that taste and standards of art are not only "objective" but are also universal, independent of time and place. W. H. Auden reflects the same position when he says that the evaluative process "demands an impersonal objective standard for judging the quality of the organization achieved."[4]

There are variations of this view that seem to permit somewhat more relative standards of art and aesthetic excellence. At another place Brooks refers to "the fixed properties of the

2. *The Well Wrought Urn* (New York, Harcourt, Brace, Harvest Books, 1947), p. 217.

3. "Criticism as Pure Speculation," in Stauffer, ed., *The Intent of the Critic*, p. 95.

4. "Criticism in a Mass Society," in Stauffer, p. 139.

poem (that is of the poem read by an ideal reader),"[5] thus shifting the idealization from poem to reader. I am not sure whether this leads to a different kind of inquiry, or merely a different focus. A genuine shift of emphasis is, however, apparent in William Wimsatt and Cleanth Brooks' discussion of the objectivity of value. "To say that a value is not objective, or not purely and simply objective, is not to say that it is not *universal,* or valid in relation to all subjects. Some such term as *inter-subjective* may perhaps be invoked to describe the accent that falls on some universals."[6] This is a major shift in the way of thinking about such a value as art, because it speaks of a distribution of experience which is a researchable topic. The same is true, in a way, of T. S. Eliot's emphasis upon value as inherent in *tradition.* Although tradition can be anything anyone wants it to be as he selectively ransacks the history of literature, still, the references are to observable phenomena, however vague the criteria may be.

The opposing view, the idea that standards are relative and preference criteria generally subjective, is set forth by Frederick Pottle. He says:

> The basic fallacy in nearly all recorded criticism is that it assumes a fixed or absolute sensibility or basis of feeling: a natural, correct basis of feeling that all right men have had since the beginning of time, or that the critic has arrived at by special grace. The view I am propounding is that an absolute basis of feeling has no more existence than an absolute frame of space. All original criticism is subjective, being a report of the impact of the work upon the critic's sensibility; all criticism is relative; and the question as to a "right" sensibility does not arise.[7]

This is certainly a clear statement, implying a different metaphysical principle, grounded not in Absolute Truth or Beauty

---

5. Quoted in Stanley E. Hyman, *The Armed Vision,* p. 276.
6. *Literary Criticism, A Short History* (New York, Knopf, 1957), p. 736.
7. *The Idiom of Poetry* (Cornell University Press, 1941), pp. 16–17.

but in the observation of the senses. While it may serve as an answer to the question "What is art?" it suggests a different process of inquiry in answer to this question, an inquiry where the definition is instrumental to a series of "why" and "how" questions.

Both positions encounter difficulties: the absolutist in answering "How do you know what this absolute quality is?" and the relativist in putting a stop to the relativism. As Brooks points out, carried to an extreme it tends to establish as many criteria as there are people, or, since a person may change his mind, as many as there are judgments.[8] In an effort to resolve this situation, and to clarify the process of formulating evaluative criteria, one may focus upon the relation between Art, or its physical embodiments, and the observer, not exclusively upon one or the other. Wimsatt and Brooks seem, at one point, to lean in this direction: "In each value situation there is both an objective and a subjective aspect—but the accent falls now upon one and now upon the other of these, and with various degrees of weight."[9] Monroe Beardsley, in a nice exposition, clarifies the difference between the type of experience we enjoy when the stimulus is internal, as in reverie or spontaneous imagination, and the experience stimulated by an external object, such as a poem.[10] This tends to put some of the subjectivism of the relativist position in a proper perspective. My own predilection would be along these relational lines, following the usual formula of social science. Most responses represent the product of an environmental stimulus and a complex of predisposing mental factors, with, as Wimsatt and Brooks say, "the accent" now falling on one, now on the other. These matters can be studied experimentally, but in the absence of experimental data they can be *thought about* in this way with a resulting conceptual clarification.

8. *The Well Wrought Urn*, pp. 227–38.
9. *Literary Criticism*, p. 736.
10. *Aesthetics, Problems in the Philosophy of Criticism*, pp. 37–38.

In some philosophical sense there may be a converging
agreement upon this relational position, with its implied empirical references and, wherever the "accent falls," a tendency
to abandon the Absolute; but in a practical operational sense,
the idea of absolute standards continues to support artistic
judgments and direct much of the critical inquiry.[11] There
are many reasons for this, one of which is the way in which
language structures thought. If it is believed that words are
exact correlatives of things and that this is inherent in the
nature of their relationship, then the very fact that there is
such a word as "Art" or "Beauty" implies that such a "thing"
exists. It then makes the greatest sense to ask "What is art?"
and to believe that there is somewhere an objective and eternal "beauty." "From the presence of the name you could argue
to the existence of the thing."[12] Indeed, you might argue that
if you manipulate the name, you manipulate the thing. It is
easy enough to see this in the accounts of primitive peoples; it
is harder to see the ways in which it is done in our own speech
and practice. Much harder to detect is the fallacy of projecting
our own experience onto the object which gives us this experience.[13] We say "it was an exciting play" or "the poem is difficult," when we mean "the play excited me and I think it will
excite others, too," or "I find the poem difficult and I think
others will, too." To go from here to the statement "the poem
is beautiful" is a short step, and hence we are led easily into
an idealistic concept of beauty as an external phenomenon
with eternal properties. It is so easy to forget that we are constantly dealing with a *relation* between observer and the thing
observed. We are touching here on the problem that Ogden

11. For example, a few pages following the discussion of value just noted
above, Wimsatt and Brooks say they do not intend to *"deny* the reality and the
value of the outer realm, the *what* which is at various levels external to each
valuing experience" (their italics, *Literary Criticism*, p. 739).

12. C. K. Ogden and I. A. Richards, *The Meaning of Meaning* (New York,
Harcourt, Brace, 1953), p. 2. My argument here is obviously based upon this
work.

13. See I. A. Richards, *Principles of Literary Criticism*, p. 20.

and Richards called "the meaning of meaning"—a problem that we shall return to later in our discussion of language; it is a central problem for literary criticism, as it is for the science of communication, and the solution is not so easy as it appeared to be to Richards.

Kenneth Burke argues that one reason for the persistence of the concept of the eternity of art and the idealistic mode is the close association of religion and art. He says:

> Noting how much of art has been a secularized variant of religious processes, particularly since the rise of the romantic reaction against capitalism and technology, we may offer a symbolical interpretation. A doctrine proclaiming the eternity of art would, from the symbolic point of view, be a natural secular analogue of a belief in the eternity of God.[14]

From its religious sources it borrows a certain eternity and commands the defenses of a religion challenged.

Another cause for the defense of the absolute may be of a psychological nature. The defense against a challenging situation is often denial. "We can say that esthetic standards being transitory, men try to compensate for this changefulness by denying its existence."[15] They simply do not see the changes in standards throughout history, or they consider these to be mere changes in language through which something consistent and eternal runs. And finally, to the philosophical, linguistic, religious, and psychological causes for the enduring quality of this view, we must add a social reason. There is a stake in the perpetuation of the view based on the occupational and ideological position of the critic, an interest arising from his existential basis. Most briefly this is again expressed by Cleanth

---

14. "The Problem of the Intrinsic as Reflected in the Neo-Aristotelian School," in *A Grammar of Motives* (New York, Prentice-Hall, 1945), p. 465. Compare Wimsatt and Brooks' view that literary theory is most satisfactorily "oriented" within the "dogma of the Incarnation." *Literary Criticism*, p. 746.
15. Burke, *Grammar of Motives*, p. 465.

Brooks who does not believe the humanities can survive without such an underpinning of objectively sustained taste. "The issue," he says, "is nothing less than the defense of the Humanities in the hard days ahead."[16]

But our problem, basically, is not to account for the persistence of an idealistic and absolutist metaphysics but to examine its results. Absolutism of the kind we have been discussing affects its apostles and followers in several ways. For one thing it is often associated with a rigid moral code, whereas a more relativistic approach permits a more flexible morality. Some rigidity here is desirable. The citizen must be able to formulate and maintain a firm morality and this must have some sanction of conscience behind it. If he should come to think that morality is entirely a matter of taste, we are lost. But the obstruction of an absolutist position to open inquiry and the use of empirical verification of the causal premises of his morality is disadvantageous for the citizen and for society. Since I cannot pretend to suggest that nice point of relativist-absolutist balance which maximizes the values of any given society, let me focus upon the intellectual, not the moral, problem.

The idea that there are absolute and unchanging qualities that make a thing beautiful, artistic, or a successful work of art leads to a strong emphasis upon certain kinds of definition and classification. As a contribution to concept clarification, this is valuable; but there is a defect in this process which, if not fatal to genuine clarity, is seriously crippling. Because the concept to be clarified is an "ideal" it need not have boundaries that can be explained in operational terms so that everyone will have the same "ideal" in his mind. Without these boundaries, the concept clarification can only go part way; hence the evaluative procedures that attempt to match individual instances against the ideal will suffer from the vague standard established. Moreover, the classification of various

16. *The Well Wrought Urn,* p. 235.

aspects of the ideal world will be confused by the vagueness of the criteria. On the other hand, a nominalist concept lends itself much more easily to clear evaluative and classificatory procedures, partly because under these circumstances "art" or "beauty" or "aesthetic object" can be defined by operational boundaries with sharp edges.

This may seem rather vague, but the truth is that not only in aesthetic discussion but also in political discussion the tendency to think of such ideas as "freedom" or "the general will" or the Hegelian "state" in the idealist mode has confused discussion since the beginning. The progressive accumulation of knowledge in the social sciences has overcome this obstacle to conceptual clarity only with difficulty, a difficulty that may possibly have been greater because of the contending usages of neighboring disciplines.

The idealist mode tends to discourage empirical research, as well as conceptual clarity, because the advantages of discovering the properties of sensory objects which but imperfectly reflect the ideals to which they are related, seem, in this perspective, to be minimal. The ideal, the absolute, and the essence, whether they are thought to be "out there" or in the mind, can only be discovered by introspective reference and the use of subjective standards of "verification." It takes a long time and many false starts to build a cumulative structure of inter-personally verified knowledge; the frame of inquiry that seeks to identify absolutes tends to discourage this. Thus, on the one hand, there is a tragic delay in the humanities in the painful effort to integrate and support theory with research findings. And, on the other hand, since one of the mental properties of the citizen that is most useful is a tendency to look for empirical evidence obtained in certain well established ways, this subjectivity may impede the exercise of a person's citizenly functions.

Inter-personal agreement can, it appears, be established over any length of time only when it is grounded either in logic or in standardized procedures which, if followed, give qualified people the same sensory experience. The idealist mode of inquiry pursues a different course and hence has led to one of the most extended instances of disagreement on record. Even the term has a history of shifting meaning which serves to confuse the discussion. No small part of the acrimony in criticism and aesthetics is due to this implicit or overt philosophical idealism and the consequent difficulty in ever finishing an argument. In the social sciences, at least, we must deplore arguments which are interminable, in a strict sense of the word.

Although not a necessary feature of an absolutist or idealist position, a tendency to reify complex "pluralities" seems associated with that view of reality. To speak of "the reader" when one means "some readers with some attributes reading some things at some times," follows easily if one is accustomed to pursue inquiries into "the beautiful," or "the fixed properties of the poem." Nothing is more likely to impede the isolation of an important cause and relationship than the use of idealized types of this kind, and nothing so encourages the natural but pernicious tendencies of the busy citizen who grasps at stereotypes, reified constructs, and other easy handles for a complex and slippery world.

The terrain of metaphysics has so many treacherous spots, I hesitate to move here without an experienced guide, but I will suggest one more source of initial error before passing on to more familiar footing. Is it not the case that literary critics often assume a world in which everything is willed, where all effects are intended effects, and where there is a confusion of purpose with function? I have the impression that this way of looking at things is given additional force by the Aristotelian origins of a certain strain of criticism, where *telos* and final causes play a part in the scheme of things which today we would treat somewhat differently.[17] In any event, unless checked this tendency will lead the inquiring student to ask

17. A related but different view is presented by Kenneth Burke in his discussion on "The Problem of the Intrinsic as Reflected in the Neo-Aristotelian School" noted above (Appendix B, *Grammar of Motives*, pp. 465–84).

about the proper, intrinsic, immanent function of a poem, rather than asking what the poem actually does to the reader. The focus upon "the intention of the work" may reflect such an Aristotelian bias. Even allowing for the ellipsis which substitutes this phrase for the "intention of the poet," we would argue that the central problem for aesthetics is better put in terms of how information about the poet modifies the poetic effect. The strong argument on the intentionalist fallacy put forward by Beardsley and Wimsatt puts this point in perspective—but theirs is an argument which must be corrected by the convincing evidence that the effect of a message is almost always influenced by information about the communicator and about the author or other source.

The citizen, adopting this intentionalist mode of inquiry, may first ask about the *telos* or purpose of a nation, and here he may find metaphoric answers with some usefulness to him. But if he goes beyond this and analyzes a constitutional system substantially in terms of the "intention" of, say, the "general welfare" or "due process" clauses of the constitution, or the intention of the framers in these respects, he will miss a great deal that is relevant for political analysis. In this case, if he were a lawyer, he would miss everything that is in the Brandeis brief.

The emphasis upon purpose rather than cause has many roots, I think, and we need not rest it entirely upon the supposed Aristotelian bias of some literary criticism. Partly, I think, it is encouraged by a confusion of the magical powers of an author over his characters (his will prevails, his purposes are sufficient) with the more limited powers of men over their own lives. Partly, no doubt, it is rooted in the affinity of religion with literature noted earlier. Partly it follows from the particular resolution of the free will controversy among many humanists. This latter point is illustrated clearly in Mr. Tate's antagonism to such terms as "drive," "stimulus," and "response"—all determinative, causal, or functional words. For these he would substitute respectively, "end," "choice," and "discrimination." The one group, he says, are "sub-rational and servile, the other rational and free."[18]

Richards says that there are only two problems for literary theory, the problem of communication and the problem of evaluation.[19] The order in which these are treated is, however, a matter of vital importance, not just as the cart and the horse have a special relation to each other, but as the waiter and the diner. The whole drift of Platonic idealism is evaluative; this is what it is all about. A major import of Aristotelianism is the analysis of whether an object fulfills its purpose, and this is evaluative. There is, I am afraid, a strong tendency to put evaluation first, prior to analysis. Robert Gorham Davis complains, "We cannot very fully or profoundly explain a story's success without knowing actually what it is that a story does."[20] But the evaluative strain, as Saintsbury and Phelps illustrate, often gets out of hand. Sentence first, verdict second —and what we shall call "literary due process" gets lost in the shuffle. And, I think, this unfortunate result, while not intended, follows from the metaphysical ground on which many critics (and often other humanists) take their stand.

18. Allen Tate, *The Man of Letters in the Modern World*, p. 17.
19. *Principles of Literary Criticism*, p. 25.
20. "Art and Anxiety," *Partisan Review, 12* (1945), 314.

3. Literary Theory and the Approach to Knowledge

THERE is no more arcane term in general use among humanists and social scientists than the term "theory." To the graduate student it carries with it a modest prestige suggesting that a person who is a theorist is brighter, deals with "deeper" and more complex material, and has insights which others who identify themselves differently do not have. The man in the street is likely to think otherwise—a theorist is for him *merely* a theorist, hence not trustworthy, and subordinate in his estimation to the pratical man of affairs. He is, of course, hardly aware of the implicit theory he himself relies upon to inform his judgments and guide his decisions. He does not know that his views on foreign affairs rest upon implicit theories of human behavior, theories of governmental action and representation, theories of the causes of war, theories of race and nationality—a world of theory probably coming consciously to his mind if at all in the form of folk sayings, proverbs, slogans, and other material of this nature. But then, he has never been taught about the nature of theory; he has been confused by his teachers to believe in the self-evident nature of "facts" and the uses of common sense explanations. Humanist and social scientist are both to blame—but the social scientists are working to correct their errors.

The social sciences only recently have developed a self-consciousness of the nature and function of theory which permits them to guide their students into the most fruitful ways of thinking about the solution to their discipline's problems.

Indeed, I think it is the case that only economics has a really central body of theory on which most of the discipline is agreed; the psychologists have at least three (Freudian, Hullian, and Lewinian) and maybe more; and I must confess that I do not think the political scientists or the sociologists have yet arrived at even this degree of consensus. But they are developing it self-consciously and with occasional small successes.

My point, then, is that to be most helpful to the citizen, and to be able to comprehend, organize, and explain its own field, a discipline should be clear about the nature of theory and the way it may be used. I sense in the field of literature a demand welling up from within for such a theoretical structure. It is almost thirty years since I. A. Richards complained "There is no other activity for which theory bears so small a proportion to practice."[1] Wellek and Warren, converging on the problem through a synthesis of disparate materials state "a sensibility can scarcely attain much critical force without being susceptible of considerable generalized, theoretical statement."[2] And Northrop Frye, in a *cri de coeur*, says:

> It occurs to me that literary criticism is now in such a state of naive induction as we find in a primitive science. Its materials, the masterpieces of literature, are not yet regarded as phenomena to be explained in terms of a conceptual framework which criticism alone possesses. They are still regarded as somehow constituting the framework or structure of criticism as well. I suggest that it is time for criticism to leap to new ground from which it can discover what the organizing or containing forms of its conceptual framework are. Criticism seems to be badly in need of a coordinating principle, a central hypothesis which, like the theory of evolution in biology, will see the phenomena it deals with as parts of a whole.[3]

1. *Practical Criticism,* p. 335.
2. *Theory of Literature,* p. 241.
3. *Anatomy of Criticism,* pp. 15–16.

Let us, for the moment at least, turn to causal theory, leaving normative theory aside until we deal with the problem of evaluation. I do not wish to be understood as saying that there is only one kind of causal theory, or that there is only one way to use such a theory; but, for purposes of exposition and with greater humility than the text will show, I will claim that a theoretical system must contain certain specified ingredients if it is to serve the purposes for which causal theory is usually employed. In the most general sense, there is only one ultimate purpose for a theory: the "explanation" or prediction of specific instances which fall in the theory's domain.[4] Its capacity in this respect is judged by three criteria: (a) the range of phenomena that it embraces, (b) the order and simplicity that it imposes on these phenomena, and (c) the power of the theory to penetrate beyond common sense and to predict, with more or less accuracy, results that are somewhat unexpected to those who do not know the theory. I might say, parenthetically, that most common senses contain mutually contradictory expectations so that, if they are queried after they know the results of research, they can claim that it is only a common sense result. If they are queried before they know the results, that is another and more embarrassing matter. We turn, then, to the ingredients of an adequate theory, and the development of these criterion ingredients in the theory of literary criticism.

In the first place a theory must have an *objective,* generally a clear specification of the phenomena that the theory is to account for. Thus the central problem for economics is said to be accounting for market value, that is, the way in which economic objects are given a price in the market place. The

4. Kenneth Burke is explicit on this point: "Induction must also use generalizations which, in effect, prophesy *before* the event. It should not be merely casuistry ready to rationalize any case after the case has occurred (a temptation to which Aristotelianism has been prone in the past). It must also risk statements as to *what to expect,* and *why.* Otherwise, such criticism becomes merely a disguised variant of impressionism, a kind of improvisation wherein the critic translates the unique imaginative sequence of the poem into a correspondingly unique conceptual equivalent." *A Grammar of Motives,* p. 473.

central focus of Hullian psychology is the explanation of
learning—how organisms, rats and men, learn. The central
focus of political science is said to be accounting for the distribution of authoritative (legal) power, the way in which
power is channeled and used. Of course the inquiries of a
discipline range afield, become descriptive, develop subsidiary
explanations, and so forth. But a theoretical system, as contrasted to its subordinate contributory theories, must have a
central focus, an explanandum, a dependent variable. And it
is crucial to note that in every case the thing explained is a
process: valuation, learning, the use of power.

I am not sure that the theory of literature has such a central
focus. It is not enough to say that the purpose of literary theory is to account for literature; for one must then ask, "What
about literature is to be accounted for?" Here I think, one
might find three answers, each of which would lead to a separate theoretical system—although they would have some relation to each other. Each is framed as a cause and effect theory,
a theory with a verb at the center. The first would be the creation of literature—a theory of creativity. This is badly needed,
and there is some work in process, although, unfortunately,
not much of it comes from the English departments of our
universities.[5] A second objective would be the explanation of
literary effects, an accounting of how literature produces
thought, feelings, and imaginative life in the readers. This I
take to be the central task of literary theory. This is a theory
of communication, essentially, an area where I. A. Richards
has made substantial contributions. We shall return to this as
our central concern, in just a moment, but first we should
mention at least the possibility that there is a third objective

5. Specifically on poetic creativity, see Robert N. Wilson, *Man Made Plain*
(Cleveland, Howard Allen, Inc., 1958), pp. 49–105; more generally, see Brewster
Ghiselin, ed., *The Creative Process* (New York, New American Library, 1957);
Jerome S. Bruner, Jacqueline J. Goodnow, and George A. Austin, *A Study of
Thinking* (New York, Wiley, 1957); Frank Barron, "Originality in Relation to
Personality and Intellect," *Journal of Personality*, 25 (1957), 730–42.

for literary theory: the explanation of the social effects of literature. This may be in the area of sociology, but much literary discussion deals with the effects of an author, say Goethe or Emerson, upon his age or subsequent ages, and many of the critics see it as their function to serve as guardians of taste and culture.[6]

The selection of the objective narrows the *framework* of the theory but does not define it. Since, following Richards and others, we have called the theory of literary effects a theory of communication, it might be instructive to look at two communication paradigms employed in other fields for other purposes. The first is Harold Lasswell's, employed, in the first instance, in the study of propaganda—a species of sub-literary reading matter with which we are not concerned. Lasswell said that the study of propaganda was a study of "Who said what to whom through what channels with what effects."[7] For purposes of the study of communications and public opinion, Berelson formulated the paradigm.

Some kinds of *communication* on some kinds of *issues*, brought to the attention of some kinds of *people* under some kinds of *conditions*, have some kinds of *effects*.[8]

This paradigm does what we said a good theoretical framework should do; it helps to *organize* the materials of a field of study. And in so doing, by specifying the main places to look for the independent variables—that is, the elements of the field which account for the changes in the objective—it helps to *define* the field of study as well. Would it be impossible,

6. On the social functions of literature see Hugh Dalziel Duncan, *Language and Literature in Society* (Chicago University Press, 1953).

7. "The Structure and Function of Communication in Society," in Lyman Bryson, ed., *The Communication of Ideas* (New York, Harper, 1948), p. 37.

8. "Communication and Public Opinion," reprinted in B. Berelson and M. Janowitz, eds., *Reader in Public Opinion and Communication* (Glencoe, Ill., The Free Press, 1950), p. 451.

then, to say that one aspect of the study of literature could be partially encompassed in the following paradigm?

> Some kinds of *literature,* having certain *structures* and *stylistic features* read (or heard) by some kinds of *readers* (or listeners) under some kinds of *conditions,* have some kinds of *effects.*

And, without examining the matter in detail, I would think it might be possible to establish a useful theoretical framework of a similar nature for the study of literary creativity.

Although the concept of a framework is more inclusive, we have been skirting around the idea of a model and this is probably the time to mention it. A model is a skeletonized conceptualization of the working relationship of the various parts of a theory. It is a paradigm in motion. Because it is skeletonized, it is never accurate, never adequately descriptive. But it shows how, if only the factors included were operative, and if the propositions were probability statements with a probabilities approaching one (except for stochastic models), and if the materials were standardized, the independent variables would account for the dependent variable or variables. In this sense it is a set of formulas, or a group of simultaneous equations. This may be offensive to some ears and I would not press the point; still, both Richards and Kenneth Burke speak of their conceptual frameworks as machines for criticism, and, in the same sense, this concept of a model does have value as an analogy if for no other reason.

Once the objective and the framework have been established the identification of specific factors or variables is necessary. Hunch, intuition, or some such element implying half-formulated theories will guide the scholar in his search for those factors he thinks will help to account for the effects he is interested in explaining. In explaining a vote decision we use such factors as candidate appeal, group identification, cross pressures, and issue orientation. In explaining the pricing decisions of a firm the economist uses concepts of marginal cost, factor cost, elasticity of demand, and so forth. Literary criticism employs the concepts of imagery, ambiguity, tension, archetypes, irony, and many more. Much of the important work of theory building is in locating the right factors, isolating them, combining them with others, identifying them, and classifying them. For many people this represents the heart of theory construction; their model in the natural sciences is botany. For unstructured material like a poem or the mind, or indeed society itself, the possibilities are limitless. But in the lexicon we have employed this is not theory but only a precursor to theory, however valuable this may be. The next step is to establish the relations which these factors may have, singly or in groups, to the qualities of the objective in which one is interested.

This is done by stating causal propositions. These are in the form of general statements about how one class of phenomena affects another class. They are empirical generalizations. They are not statements about particular men, poems, events; or at least we shall not use the term proposition in this way. Gresham's law is a familiar example: cheap money tends to drive out dear; or again, frustration is always (or tends to be) followed by aggression; power tends to corrupt power holders; metaphors tend to derive their poetic power from their inclusion of both the universal and the particular in the same symbol. These propositions always imply a *ceteris paribus* statement; obviously the influence of some important extraneous influence on the effect to be explained will vitiate the proposition. Most propositions in the social sciences, moreover, are probability statements because even under the best circumstances we cannot control all the factors that might influence the result—hence the "tend to" form of the statements.

The explanation of a particular result, the peculiar effects of a given poem on most readers, for example, or the effects of some part of a poem, some special image, are explained by subsuming the particular under the general in a syllogistic fashion, thus:

(All)True paradox contributes to the sense of "pleasant surprise" in a reader.

Wordsworth's sonnet "Composed upon Westminster
Bridge" is a true paradox (revealing the author's surprise at the natural beauty of artificial man-made London seen in the early morning light).

The true paradox in Wordsworth's sonnet contributes to
the reader's sense of "pleasant surprise" when he reads
the poem.

I have adapted this rather freely from Cleanth Brooks' analysis of "The Language of Paradox,"[9] and although there will
be those who think I have wrenched a prosaic statement out
of a fine piece of writing, I think the sense is substantially
correct. I am not stating at all that criticism should be written
this way—on this point I infinitely prefer Brooks to Lane—
but I am saying in developing a theory of literature the logic
of the situation should be *thought of* in this way.

Finally, a theory, as I have employed the term, will articulate the specific propositions, such as the one about paradox
above, into a system of propositions such that they interlock
and support one another. Thus a theory of business cycles is
made up of propositions about liquidity preference, inventory
depletion, the leverage principle, and other similar matters.
Theories of neurosis include sub-theories of the Oedipal situation, repression, fixation, and so on. And, as we shall show,
Richards' theory of poetic effects represents an articulation of
a number of theories of imagery, rhythm, and individual psychology.

It may have appeared from our discussion that it would not
be possible to have theories in a field without some over-arch-
ing framework with some central objective at its head. This is
clearly not the case. One can have a theory of legislative decision making without a theory of "the authoritative allocation
of power"; one can have a theory of migration without a gen-

9. *The Well Wrought Urn*, p. 5.

eral demographic theory; and so forth. As we pursue our endeavors, each of us more or less alone, we bite off a little more than we can chew easily, and try with what theories we can devise, to make sense of our material. William Wimsatt and Cleanth Brooks speak of a "theory of irony," and of a "metaphoric theory of poetics," the latter being characterized as "almost necessarily a theory of multiple focuses and hence a historic theory and a perspective theory."[10] There is ample evidence in their review of the history of criticism of a variety of *approaches* to the study of literature in which are embedded a variety of these smaller and specialized theories. Rich, insightful, and penetrating as they are, they do not in their present form permit their users to employ them to explain individual cases, that is, to subsume these cases under general statements of relationships. They form the materials for excellent specialized theories, but they are not themselves theories. This is not a detractor's statement; the insight and imagination—surely as much a part of analysis as formal theorizing—is so exciting that an outsider can only wish that some aspects of his own field might be illuminated in a similar way.

In the humanities generally, just as in the social sciences, the dawning consciousness of the importance of how knowledge is structured has brought a number of people to try their hand at formulating theories or even theories of theory. Let us, then, sample a few in the theory of literature. Monroe Beardsley has written the best current work in this field, but, as a philosopher and logician, he stands a little outside the world I am dealing with.[11] Richard McKeon sets the stage with an interpretation of what he terms "modes" of aesthetic analysis.[12] There are six of these, each with its own "variables

10. *Literary Criticism, A Short History*, pp. 747, 750.

11. See his *Aesthetics, Problems in the Philosophy of Criticism.*

12. "The Philosophic Bases of Art and Criticism" in R. S. Crane, ed., *Critics and Criticism* (abridged edition, University of Chicago Press, Phoenix Books, 1957), pp. 258–65.

and constants" and terms of analysis. The first of these is the *dialectical,* which consists, as its name suggests, of setting in opposition to each other various ingredients of an analytical structure. These may be a dialectic of "things" as where Plato sets the objects imitated against the imitation, or a dialectic of knowledge, as where Kant opposes natural philosophy to moral philosophy. A second mode is the *scientific,* which is illustrated by the Aristotelian method of analysis of ends and efficient causes, the classification of forms, and the problem of unity and structure.

The *poetic* mode is the third; it relies upon an analysis of the way great authors have conceptualized and expressed their material, leading from there to classification of the poetic art. In this sense it is Coleridgean. A fourth mode is called the *scholarly* mode. It goes directly to the particular authors and analyzes them in their historical and particular contexts, leading to a history of evaluation. The *technical* mode, a fifth variety, refers to the way in which audiences respond and back, then, to the devices, structures, and forms which evoke these responses. Finally, sixth, the *formal* mode focuses upon the poetic works themselves and their component elements, with a classification of styles and languages as means of communication.

Now I have not done justice to McKeon's analysis in this brief description, but I think it is fair to say that none of these embody the concept of theory outlined above. In spite of the reference to "variables and constants" one would be hard put to it to specify dependent and independent variables in these modes, to isolate and classify propositions, to formulate a theoretical structure which would permit one to explain or predict poetic effects or creativity, or to design a research procedure that would permit the testing of the propositions.

Northrop Frye represents a quite different approach to the concept of the appropriate nature of a theory of literature. What Frye would like is some embracing theory which would include everything in an appropriate structure. His ideal is a mathematical theory, relying on the syntactical, symbolic, and significative features of language to serve as the basis of such a theory. He says:

> Both literature and mathematics proceed from postulates, not facts; both can be applied to external reality and yet exist also in a "pure" or self-contained form. Both, furthermore, drive a wedge between the antithesis of being and non-being that is so important for discursive thought. . . . Other points in this analogy strike one: the curious similarity in form, for instance, between the units of literature and of mathematics, the metaphor and the equation. Both of these are, in the expanded sense of the term employed by many logicians, tautologies. But if the analogy is to hold, the question of course arises: is literature like mathematics in being substantially useful, and not just incidentally so?[13]

It is an interesting idea. Certainly the notion of mathematical models in the social sciences has attracted considerable interest of late, and in economics and psychology their development has been deemed quite successful. But it should be observed that these efforts are made within the context of disciplines that have established rigorous criteria for verification, either observational or experimental. Without this check, mathematical theories tend to become increasingly "autistic," that is concerned with the rules of logic and consistency, rather than with the usefulness for explaining or predicting or even relevance to specific instances of the phenomena with which they are concerned.

Perhaps, then, the place to look is not in the theories of theory, but in the applied theories that have been developed. Wellek and Warren, Wimsatt and Brooks, and I. A. Richards may serve as examples.

13. *Anatomy of Criticism*, pp. 351–52.

In their *Theory of Literature* Wellek and Warren state that they have "sought to unite 'poetics' (or literary theory) and 'criticism' (evaluation of literature) with 'scholarship' ('research') and 'literary history' (the 'dynamics' of literature, in contrast to the 'statics' of theory and criticism)." It is not a mere reproduction of the views of others but has instead been "written from a consistent point of view."[14] Because of its inclusive character it deals with a definition of the field and delineation of literature and art, the function of literature, the comparative aspects of the field, the relation of literature to biography, psychology, society, and other arts, and then, after dealing with some of the problems of scholarship and texts, plunges into that portion of the study of literature which brings it closest to the idea of theory we have outlined above. Here, under a heading of "the intrinsic study of literature" (a heading which raises questions of a fundamental order), the authors deal with euphony, rhythm, and meter; style and stylistics; image, metaphor, symbol, myth; narrative fiction; literary genres; evaluation. They then conclude with literary history.

If, as the authors state, "the two main organizing principles of poetry . . . are meter and metaphor" the chapter on "Image, Metaphor, Symbol, Myth" should include an important part of the theoretical discussion. This chapter, like the others in this work, is a miracle of lucidity, beautifully organized, learned and wise. After a brief discussion of the relation of the four terms (discovering two factors in them, sensuousness and figurative or oblique speech) the authors take up each of the four concepts in turn. In each case they "place" the term by showing something about its non-poetic uses, discuss the various ideas of the nature of the concept in the works of a variety of writers, classify the types which they distinguish or which others have, suggest the essential elements in the concept, discriminate among these, and, in some cases, show how myth or

14. *Theory of Literature*, p. v.

metaphor, or image, or symbol has been used. In a few cases
they give an illustration and an analysis of the function of the
metaphor or other device in a poem. Toward the end of the
chapter they devote some time to a seven-fold typology of
imagery by Henry Wells and a two-fold typology by Herman
Pongs. Finally there is some discussion of the way imagery
reveals the nature of the poet's psyche, and some subtler uses
of imagery to reveal a new level of meaning in Shakespeare.
This is, broadly speaking, an analysis of types, of uses, of distinctions; it consists of comparisons and discriminations, illustrations, some judgments, and much careful reporting.

Buried throughout the whole wonderful assemblage of
ideas and judgments, there is an enormous amount of theory;
but it is latent, hard to isolate, implicit. Here and there, the
"archeologist" in search of theory finds a protruding limb. For
example, if I may paraphrase and tidy up and perhaps extend
the meanings a trifle:[15]

> The efficacy of an image is a function not so much of its
> "vividness" as of its "character as a mental event pe-
> culiarly connected with sensation." (Richards)
> The efficacy of an image is a function of its "unification
> of disparate ideas." (Pound)
> The efficacy of an image is a function more of its visual
> quality than of its auditory quality. (Eliot)

These are propositions relating "efficacy of imagery" to qualities of language, ideas, and the psychology of the reader. If
efficacy were somehow specified the propositions would gain
in value, but they are useful as they stand.

In Wimsatt and Brooks' monumental "short" history of
literary criticism these authors, like Wellek and Warren,
maintain a consistent point of view, finding a continuity and
reciprocity among the critics of all ages that gives the field
unity and a common focus. This situation, it would appear, is

15. *Theory of Literature*, p. 176.

ideal for the theorist in that he does not then have an indefinite number of explananda to worry about; the plurality comes to a focus at the end. The body of the work is a history and analysis of ideas about literature and hence is an analytic history of literary theories and includes, as Wellek and Warren did, an enormous number of half-buried propositions, but these are inchoate, discrete, and, although criticized, never systematically reconciled. At the end, there is some drawing together of themes and several important analytic discussions of a theory of evaluation, a theory of the relation between poetry and emotional life, and some comments on the essential ingredients of criticism. In three pages, there is an effort to focus upon "some comprehensive issue, some paradoxical junction, that will catch, if only in a precarious and momentary stasis, the whole of the problem."[16] The central theoretical notion that emerges from this discussion is the idea expressed in McKeon's first mode—dialectic, or, more accurately, equilibrium. "A theory of art will not be able to get along without at least two key terms—to stand in partial opposition to each other and to keep the theory from collapsing into tautology, or into literalism."[17] In one instance the antinomy is established between sensory values and spiritual values, with the function of criticism stated as keeping art in the middle, pursuing an aesthetic value which either balances or combines these two in paradox and metaphor. More fundamentally, the partial antithesis is established between *making,* which is associated with Aristotle, and a combination of *saying* and *seeing,* which are associated with Plato. These suggest a range of opposite pairs which are somehow embraced by the basic "making" versus "saying-seeing" opposites: drama vs. statement, metaphor vs. literal fact, concrete vs. abstract, and so forth.[18]

---

16. *Literary Criticism,* p. 752.
17. Ibid., p. 753.
18. Ibid., pp. 753–55.

This seems to be a good start; it seems consonant with other great theories which have used dialectical or equilibrium analysis: the Marxian theory of class relationships; the Freudian theory of the tension among the id, the ego, and the super-ego; and the economists' antithesis between supply and demand. But on closer inspection it appears that there is a vital difference. The Marxist theory explains a process with specified end results: the *changing* power and relationship of social classes; the Freudian theory deals with the *development* of neurosis or of personality; economic theory explains the *fixing* of a price. But the Wimsatt-Brooks theory states a tension present in literature, a condition of art. "Art or poetry is the peculiar situation where we see each member of each pair only in or through its opposite: making through saying and saying through making."[19] Stating a condition of art is not explaining the end result of a process. To be comparable, the theory would have to be recast so as to offer a framework for the explanation of the results of art, that is, the effect on the reader of art, if you like, the artistic process as it is received by its consumer. I cannot say that this recasting is desirable in the interests of literary criticism (though I think it probably is); but if the aim is to establish a theory which fulfills the conditions of a good theoretical structure, that is, the explanation of certain specified phenomena, then, perhaps this recasting has merit.

There are other, indeed many, "theories" of literature or theories of criticism (they seem to merge into each other): Kenneth Burke, early in his career developed what he calls a "machine for criticism" but as he points out, "It is a kind of judgment machine, designed to serve as an instrument for clarifying critical issues (not so much for settling issues as for making the nature of a controversy more definite)."[20] It is, then, not a theory with general propositions, under which specific instances may be subsumed in the interest of predic-

19. Ibid., p. 753.
20. *Counter-Statement,* p. v. The first edition was published in 1931.

tion or explanation. His pentad, developed later, is, likewise, a set of interrelated factors to be taken into account, perhaps even a framework or paradigm in the specific sense employed above, but there are very few propositions and their architecture is not clear.

There are, in fact, two theories of literature as communication which come close to fulfilling the formal criteria we set forth at the outset. One is Tolstoy's—a reminder that the fulfillment of formal criteria is not a substitute for sensibility, or that the concept of communication (he calls it "infection") is not one of Arnold's or anybody else's touchstones to critical understanding. Tolstoy has a clear focus on what is to be explained; he identifies the factors he thinks are relevant; he propositionalizes in a formal sense, however cloudy the language ("the infectiousness of art depends . . . on the greater or lesser individuality of the feeling transmitted"); and he understands that each of these factors contributes a part to a final accounting of his objective.[21] But the model is inadequate.

Richards, apparently, is our man. He is a giant figure in the history of criticism; in Wimsatt and Brooks he is taken as the representative spokesman for one of three forms of criticism—the other two are Aristotle and Croce. He seems, in some ways, to be considered "the opposition" by a wide range of critics including Auden, Ransom, and Tate. His influence on the development of linguistics, aesthetics, and education, as well as literary criticism, has been substantial. I do not care to base my views of the study of literature upon the acceptance of Richardian doctrine; I think these views will stand independently, but that there is some congruence must already have become apparent.

21. *What is Art? and Essay on Art,* trans. Aylmer Maude for the Tolstoy Society (London, Oxford University Press, 1929), p. 288. But notice this curious invitation to science: "Possibly in the future science may reveal to art yet newer and higher ideals which art may realize; but in our time the destiny of art is clear and definite. The task of Christian art is to establish brotherly union among men." Ibid., p. 288.

Richards, as we have said, is primarily concerned with two processes: the process of communication and the process of evaluation. No little part of the success of his theory is due to the fact that he focuses upon process, rather than upon an object, such as the poem or the ultimate value. His analysis of process has all the essential ingredients of a theory. The objective of his communication analysis is the effect produced in the mind of the reader. He is successful in identifying and analyzing the way this objective may be accounted for because he recognizes that it is, in fact, plural—there are many kinds of minds; each mind brings special qualities to the experience, and there are, therefore, many kinds of effects and meanings. The framework approaches adequacy at least for his time; indeed, he constructs something similar to the paradigm we mentioned earlier. In his chapter on "The Analysis of a Poem,"[22] he gives a theory of the way in which a stimulus, such as the word "cloud," produces (a) visual sensations, (b) tied imagery, that is, imagery which is more or less standard for that word, (c) free imagery, which is dependent upon the idiosyncratic associations of the reader, (d) references, or thoughts about things giving the sense meaning of the word and phrase. These mental products then become linked with an emotional complex which is part of the personality of the reader and which becomes activated and quasi-conscious when the visual sensations of the word are set in motion. These emotions, in turn, produce a set of attitudes which may be articulated and are a temporary end product of the poetic experience. Of course this is crude—but it is a start and permits further analysis in greater detail and depth. The paradigm introduced does not include many of the facets of the stimulus—but the analysis does, and so the framework is enlarged to deal with rhythm and meter, allusion, form, relations to reality, and much more.

Richards, of course, does not reduce his theory to a set of

22. *Principles of Literary Criticism*, pp. 114–33.

propositions, but, because of the clarity of his theoretical structure and his focus upon process, they are not difficult to descry. For example:[23]

> Rhythm and its specialized form, meter, depend upon repetition, and expectancy.

With its corollary:

> The effect produced by what actually follows [reading a line of verse] depends very closely upon this unconscious preparation, and consists largely of the further twist it gives to expectancy.

Or, the following propositions taken together:

> The way in which the sound of a word is taken varies with the emotion already in being.

> The sound of words comes to its full power only through rhythm.

Or:

> Those [rhythms] which are too easily "seen through" grow cloying or insipid unless hypnoidal states intervene.

It would be a simple matter, with hardly any change in grammar, to convert these sentences into easily recognizable propositions. Propositions are no substitute for arguments and more elaborate explications; they are summaries, for easier use and manipulation—and always to be employed as modified by this explication and by cognate propositions. Only the obscurantist, or the neophyte in the uses of theory is likely to mistake this matter.

---

23. *Principles*, pp. 135, 137, 138. I am aware that some critics think Richards changed his mind on a number of critical matters when he wrote *The Philosophy of Rhetoric* (1936). If so, I stand with the earlier Richards; but it is not clear that he did change.

Why is it that the best critic in the business, Mr. Cleanth Brooks, whose works are a delight to read and a revelation of what reading a poem can be like, does not rely on an explicit interlocking propositional theory such as those employed in other disciplines?[24] Why can Wellek and Warren say of Lowes:

> In *The Road to Xanadu*, Lowes reconstructs with the acumen of a brilliant detective the process of association by which the vastly and curiously read Coleridge moved from one quotation or allusion to another. As for theory, however, he is soon content: a few purely figurative terms serve him to describe the creative process.[25]

And why can Ransom say of Eliot, whom he greatly admires: "There is in Eliot's writings an immediate critical sense which is expert and infallible, but it consists with a theoretical innocence."[26] It is an old question, one which is somewhat wearying to a political scientist who has never carried a precinct. The relation of theory to practice, although important, cannot be explored here, only the *lacunae* noted.

But it might be useful to make several observations. First, let us note that virtuosity in any field is often divorced from theoretical knowledge: the pianist and musical theory; Goebbels and the theory of propaganda; even in psychoanalysis, the best clinician is rarely the best theorist. None of this, in these fields, is thought to vitiate the importance of theory and I don't see why it should in literary analysis.

In the second place, not all critics are virtuosi, hence Paul Lazarsfeld's parable of the centipede is relevant:

24. *Understanding Poetry* (with Robert Penn Warren; New York, Henry Holt, 1950), is an extraordinary guide to poetry but not a satisfactory empirically based theory of poetic effect, for the reasons I have outlined above.

25. *Theory of Literature*, p. 77.

26. *The New Criticism*, p. 145.

There is a well-known story about the centipede who lost his ability to walk when he was asked in which order he moved his feet. But other details of the story are buried in conspiratorial silence. First of all, there is no mention of the fact that the inquiry came from a methodologist who wanted to improve the walking efficiency of the centipede community. Then little attention is paid to the other centipedes who participated in the investigation. . . . Some were able to give rather reasonable answers; from these the investigator worked diligently to arrive at general principles of walking behavior. . . . Of course, the great centipede ballet dancer and other creative artists continued to depend upon hereditary endowments, and could not be produced by the school system. But the general level of walking, characteristic of the centipede in the street, was improved. In this way, individuals endowed with great personal gifts started out at a higher level, and achieved creative performance unparalleled in the past.[27]

Third, I think there is a contribution to understanding which only the theorist can make, a contribution beyond the range of the expert critic. Let me see if the following example is persuasive. In his discussion of Swinburne, Eliot probes into a number of crevices, finds many of his faults and makes some comparisons, most of them somewhat to the detriment of Swinburne. He comes to the question of the relation of words to the thoughts and to the emotions which they evoke and hits happily upon the idea that "It is the word that gives him the thrill, not the object."[28] He fails to go through the word to the objective referent and hence the effects have no "meaning"

---

27. *The Language of Social Research* (Glencoe, Ill., The Free Press, 1955), p. 1.

28. T. S. Eliot, *The Sacred Wood* (London, Methuen, University Paperbacks, 1960), p. 148.

to support them. It is a good point, but we stop short of an understanding of the principles at work.

In his chapter on "The Analysis of a Poem" in which he sets forth his famous diagrammatic presentation, Richards makes a related point, very close to Eliot's but not the same. Quoting a stanza from Swinburne's "Before the Mirror," he says: "Little beyond vague thoughts of the things the words stand for is here required. They do not have to be brought into intelligible connection with one another." This is "mere sense without any further reflection."[29] Again, one agrees; the words do have their original single meanings—this they have as well as sounds. What makes Richards' discussion a better explanation than Eliot's is the fact that his insight fits into a framework which accounts for just exactly the Swinburnian way of communicating emotion: an emphasis on free imagery with relatively few "references" or cognitive processes which link one word to another in a phrase with meaning. The theory provides for an emotional response on the basis of single word imagery, but it is impoverished in a way that is clearly conceptualized in the theory. I am not offering this as a substitute for literary criticism of the usual kind; it supplements, enriches, and gives meaning to the statements which such criticism embodies.

I am assuming in this brief excursion into the scope and methods of the humanities, chiefly the study of literature, that the habits of mind developed in one discipline are likely to persist and to be applied elsewhere, that the distinctions in method appropriate for thinking and talking about *The Brothers Karamazov* and for the Politburo are often exaggerated, that the influence of teachers transcends their subject matter, and that as life hurries by one draws on what comes easily to hand in an effort to cope with it. If this is the case, the kind of mental training students get in the universities is

29. *Principles of Literary Criticism,* p. 129.

a matter of some importance to the manner in which men grasp the political and social events of their adult years. Essentially what we have said above is that most of the theory of literary criticism, as a sample of theoretical thinking in the humanities, is not properly a theory at all and hence fails to show students or others how to find and grapple with the underlying causal premises of their own thinking. And, further, that a love of systematic and orderly thinking necessary to tackle these problems in a sympathetic manner is not widespread.

But perhaps these have no real relevance to the problems of the citizen. Let us see. What is required in this situation is some close textual analysis of citizen thought—a rather difficult task since citizen thought, even more than literature, is hard to sample. But, since we are concerned with education as well as citizen thought, we may look at some material in a college newspaper with which I am familiar. I am sampling the better statements, not the "boners" and my purpose is not to expose error but to illustrate the possible relevance of the points made above. Here are several sentences taken from a column of commentary on the Soviet Union.

> It is true that Khrushchev has demonstrated a desire to avoid terror and unmitigated violence as instruments of policy. In contrast to the Stalinist regime where extreme repression was pursued without any regard to political necessity, the present leadership seems to recognize that terror holds grave risks for those who employ it. Under Stalin no one was safe from liquidation. Furthermore today's Soviets are not so constituted as to enjoy political murder for its own sake. The events in Hungary, however, show that Khrushchev and his associates will sanction the most brutal expedients to preserve the interests of communism as they conceive them. If the system of order under which they hold power is threatened, everything is permissible in the interests of maintaining it.

As speculative reporting, or commenting on the passing scene goes, this is not bad. Let us consider it to be one of T. S. Eliot's less adequate "remarks" or perhaps an "insight" into the situation. It certainly is not political or social theory and at first glance it does not seem to embody much theory; but that is probably because we are not trained to have that deft ear for theoretical premises comparable to our ear for the meanings of ambiguity and metaphor. But if we approach it more closely we see that there is a tendency to personalize the decisions of the Soviet Government, and to emphasize the personal emotions and attitudes of the leaders (e.g. "desire," "recognize [personal] risks," "enjoy," etc.), and it appears that the key to Soviet policy is to know what these men want to do and how they see the situation with respect to "maintaining" "the system of order under which they hold power." Already a number of specialized motives have been mentioned, but the problem is more complex.

Daniel Bell, a sociologist, has written a piece with a Pirandello title, "Ten Theories in Search of Reality."[30] It is about explaining and predicting Soviet behavior. In the first place, it seems, there are the characterological theories, emphasizing the persistent strains and themes in Russian behavior which have emerged as a product of their culture, particularly the character forming influences of childhood and youth. These are of two kinds, the theories that deal generally with the Russian character historically, and those, like that of Nathan Leites, that deal with the governing elite. There are several sociological theories. One of these emphasizes the social system, including the chronic tendency to "overcommitment of resources," and the concentration of authority as major influences on what the Soviet Government will or can do. Another emphasizes the "ideal types" and focuses on the several ways power is and has been transmitted in the Soviet Union and suggests the several paths of probable development of

30. *World Politics*, *10* (1958), 327–65.

power relations. As one might expect, there are Marxist theories of Soviet behavior and development, a kind of dialectic between the dictatorship of the proletariat and the emerging new centers of power. Another theory, also Marxist, is that the "normal" evolution of exploitation and revolution is taking place in the Soviet Union, which is no longer a communist state. Hence foreign affairs may be guided by the growing revolutionary charge within the state. There are theories of the eventual unfolding of all dictatorships which place the Soviet Union in a certain class of dictatorships and at a certain stage of development. There is something Bell calls "Kremlinology"—perhaps this is the closest analogy to the quotation employed above. There are those who look to the Slavic history and institutions that underlie the Soviet System to see what will be the course of action. And finally there is the geopolitical school of analysis with relevant comments on Soviet interests in Hungary.

These theories are hardly of equal worth or equal relevance to the topic treated in the quotation. What is more, they are not all cast in the form we outlined earlier; they are, for the most part, vague, "literary," anecdotal, and rarely expressed in propositional form. We do not employ them to illustrate theoretical precision; they illustrate something else. They illustrate the importance of a continuous, searching, and systematic examination of the theoretical premises of an insight, hunch, or common-sense reporting of fact. Unless the student or citizen is theory conscious, looking for more basic principles and generalizations to inform his thinking and suggest alternate ways of looking at something to be accounted for, he will merely report the news and comment on it; he will not be able to analyze it in any meaningful sense.

4. Types and Classification

BEFORE 1859 when Darwin published his *The Origin of the Species,* there had been elaborate work by Linnaeus and later by Lamarck and others in the classification and description of the various biological types. This classification, although revolutionized by Darwinian concepts, was essential in the development of the concept of evolution; it provided a structure for the phenomena and gave clues for what to look for. The fact that Wallace came independently to an evolutionary theory in the same year is supporting evidence for this view. Taxonomy, morphology, anatomy, while related to function, often precede the development of functional analysis and are essential to that development. This is certain to be the case in the study of literature.

And it is also the case in the study of society. The point I seek to establish here is that in any discipline a failure to embody and accept the canons of clear and fruitful conceptualization, definition, and classification serves to retard the development of learning in that discipline (in this case, literary criticism) and, moreover, extends this retardation to other areas of thought (in this case, social and political thought). Classification is a creative act—or can be such. "The devising of a classification . . . involves speculation and theorizing." The payoff is not simply in ordering the field neatly, but, as Julian Huxley says, in the "number of prophecies and deductions it makes possible."[1] If one must choose between a crea-

---

1. "Towards the New Systematics," in J. Huxley, ed., *The New Systematics* (Oxford University Press, Eng., 1940), p. 20, as quoted in Carl G. Hempel, "Fundamentals of Concept Formation in Empirical Science," *International Encyclopedia of Unified Science,* 2, No. 7 (1952), 53. The following discussion relies in part on Hempel's article.

tive type of classification productive of interesting ideas, and a neat one with few boundary problems, clearly the imaginative one is to be preferred. Still, creativity could be hampered by confusion, indistinctness, and ambiguity—the standards of a good classificatory system should be kept in mind.[2]

These standards can be summarized somewhat as follows. A logical system will establish in a domain or area a series of classes or sets which are exhaustive and mutually exclusive. That is, nothing is left out, and nothing could belong to two classes at once. If the classification purports to describe an empirical world, then the classification also includes statements about the way the real world "naturally" clusters and therefore implies some empirical laws. The distinction sometimes made between a "natural classification" and an "artificial classification" reminds us that classifications are either better or worse for the purposes at hand which, in turn, focuses attention on the ultimate criterion: "Is the classification the most fruitful one for thinking about, accounting for, and predicting from a body of phenomena?"

In order to minimize ambiguity about marginal cases the boundaries between classes should be as sharp and clear as possible, a feature which usually comes from precise definition and clear conceptualization. Definition, then, which we treat briefly in our discussion of language, deserves the most careful attention in establishing a classificatory system. Most classificatory criteria, such as "centralization of authority" or "ambiguity" or even "unity" are not simply "either/or" attributes, but are "more or less" attributes, hence the problem of establishing a cutting-off point on a continuum, which, in turn, implies the use of an explicit (or, more likely, an implicit) metric of some kind. In general, the principle to follow is to establish such cutting-off points between the modes, where

2. One way in which rigid standards of classification improve creativity is shown in Allen Barton, "The Concept of Property-Space in Social Research," in Paul F. Lazarsfeld and Morris R. Rosenberg, *The Language of Social Research* (Glencoe, Ill., The Free Press, 1955), pp. 40–53.

the cases are the fewest in number and the marginalia problem, therefore, the smallest. If a metric is not available, a simple ordering of phenomena, employing a set of (transitive) comparisons is suitable. In either event, precise classification, and therefore precise thinking, is encouraged by stipulating where on the continuum employed an item leaves one class and enters another. It is in this area of relational or functional specification that Aristotelian systems of classification are least likely to be satisfactory. Classification, like criticism, is not autotelic.

The interrelationship of the attributes of the items classified may call for special examination, as the word "syndrome" suggests. Thus it may be if one thinks of types of imagery, for example, the qualities of auditory sensation, emotionality, and cognitive reference may all have a special interlocking relationship to each other, perhaps they all reflect some more basic quality, or perhaps they each imply the other in some causal sense. Typologies are usually constructed on the basis of some such interactive relation among the elements with which the typology deals. Classificatory systems should be economical; the fewer the classes the easier it is to work with them.

In the social sciences, at least, classificatory systems are long since completely out of hand; they run riot, everyone tends to develop his own, master the special language associated with his types, and, thus fortified, defend his empire with a verbal facility and forensic zeal which becomes in time quite forbidding. Unfortunately, I do not think the humanities are much better. Much of the difficulty rests on the confusion of language, a matter to which we shall return, but there are other difficulties. Wellek and Warren mention that there are some lists of types of figures used in literature itemizing two hundred and fifty types, lists which others have reduced to two or three.[3] Clearly the principles of economy and adequacy have been given different weights in this matter. Later, in their

3. *Theory of Literature*, p. 183.

discussion of genres, and in dealing with the period most serious about the importance of these classifications, they say: "if
we look to Neo-Classical criticism for definition of genre or
method of distinguishing genre from genre, we find little consistency or even awareness of the need for a rationale."[4] De-
feated by similar considerations, apparently Croce gave up
the search for fundamental categories and used labels as he
liked. Another solution of sorts, with equally bad results, is
to make no distinctions at all, lumping all readers together as
"the reader" and all poets together as "the poet"—not simply
for convenience but for want of conceptual differentiation.

But the problem of establishing a classificatory system that
will persuade everyone that it is a natural system, in the sense
that it differentiates among the phenomena in the ways most
useful for analysis, is only one of the important problems. Another equally important problem is the way in which such
classifications are employed in attempting explanations of individual literary works, that is, in the critical process. Richard
McKeon finds that, however they have been devised, the classificatory terms employed have been abused. He refers dispar-
agingly to such terms as

> realism, nominalism, conceptualism, or dogmatism, skep-
> ticism, criticism, or idealism, materialism, naturalism,
> and so through the dreary list of tags by which significant
> explanations are reduced to props for one or more expla-
> nations that will in turn be honored and dismissed with
> a technical name.[5]

Stanley Hyman registers his disgust in the same vein:

> Except for Empson and the little work derived from
> his, almost all contemporary categorical criticism has
> been the use of the category to evade analysis—that is,

4. Ibid., p. 219.

5. "The Philosophic Bases of Art and Criticism," in Crane, ed., *Critics and
Criticism*, p. 251.

"pigeon-holing." At its worst, this is the easy formulation of reviewing, the mechanical and meaningless use of such terms as "romantic," "classical," "realist," "naturalist," and is an odd tradition in an otherwise literary history which we might call the Lofty Chapter Heading.[6]

But still, there are many meaningful classes, genres, types, versions, and other discriminated groupings of the material examined. From the classes based on the rule of the author (speaker) in the classical vein—lyric, epic, and dramatic—to Wimsatt and Brooks' five-fold distinction: dramatic, epistolary, heroic, burlesque, and lyric, the variety of classifications generally shows some meaningful struggle to sort literature out in such a way as to make sense to the interpreters of the time.[7] Both the effort and the problem are reflected in William Empson's attempts to classify his *Seven Types of Ambiguity:*

> Thus I think my seven types form an immediately useful set of distinctions, but to a more serious analyst they would appear trivial and hardly to be distinguished from one another. I call them useful, not merely as a means of stringing examples, but because, in complicated matters, any distinction between cases, however irrelevant, may serve to heighten one's consciousness of the cases themselves.[8]

No doubt this is true, and well said, but still, inasmuch as Empson admits that his first type seems to cover all the cases, he suffers from his confused criteria. Others did, too. Beardsley says of Empson, "His attempt to classify these nuances in seven categories broke down—no one could really follow the distinctions or apply them himself."[9] Perhaps complete clarity

6. *The Armed Vision*, p. 258.
7. *Literary Criticism, A Short History*, pp. 750–51.
8. *Seven Types of Ambiguity* (New York, Meridian Books, 1955), p. 286.
9. *Aesthetics, Problems in the Philosophy of Criticism*, p. 151.

in these matters is impossible, but closer attention to the criteria of a good classificatory scheme would certainly help. The
preference for connotative language with multiple or vague
referents tends to create classes with blurred distinctions; the
lack of a commonly agreed upon criterion of what is to be
explained tends to multiply the number of classificatory
schemes until they become difficult to manage; and the lack
of any part of the discipline concerned with Bridgman's op-
erationalizing concept tends never to bring the terms into a
situation where they must, in order to be successful, mean the
same thing to all observers.

Classification, like definition, is rarely as interesting as theory building, but in some sense it must precede it. In political
science we have an ancient tradition of classifying governmental forms into threes: timocracy, oligarchy, and democracy, or monarchy, aristocracy, and republic. More recently
there has been introduced into this classificatory scheme the
distinctions between various dictatorial regimes, particularly
old-fashioned or Napoleonic types, and the totalitarian types
represented by the Nazi and the Communist regimes. Some of
the problems of erecting a classificatory system of this kind, as
well as the problems of classifying specific cases, may be illustrated by a sentence from the comment on Soviet policy in the
student paper referred to earlier. The author speaks first of
some liberalizing changes in the Soviet Union. He then says:
"Nonetheless their cumulative effect is insufficient to alter the
essentially totalitarian nature of Soviet Communism."

Mental clarity in this instance would require the student
and citizen to be roughly familiar with the following ideas implied in his statement. In the first place he should be aware of
the classificatory system he has employed, that is, he should be
aware of the alternative classes of state systems in which he
might have put Soviet communism. Is he classifying Soviet
communism as totalitarian, in contrast to Napoleonic dictatorship, or in contrast to democracy and, if the latter, does he,
as some do, make the distinction between a democracy and a

republic? These questions, in turn, will depend upon the criteria he has employed for his classificatory system. Do they include the decentralization of authority, the sharing of decision-making power among certain groups, the degree of control over opinion-formation, the freedom of dissent available to the public or to certain portions, degree of constitutional restraints on the government, and so forth?

Once he has established the classificatory system of which totalitarianism is a part, and the criteria employed in differentiating its elements, he may want to examine these criteria with greater care. For example, his comment about the "cumulative effect" of the liberalizing changes suggests the following possibilities: (a) these changes all occurred along one "liberalism" dimension, such that they were changes of degree on one continuum, the only important one for the classificatory scheme, or (b) that there are several dimensions and criteria, and that they are collectively covered by the "liberalism" concept, but may in fact be somewhat independent of each other. If (b) is the case, the question (c) arises: can one achieve the "totalitarianism" classification with high scores on any one of these several criterion dimensions, or is it necessary to have high scores on several of them?

The use of the phrase "essentially totalitarian" suggests that there are degrees of totalitarianism and that hence the entire class, as well as the criteria for membership in the class, is one of not "either/or" but "more or less."

Finally, there may be some questions about the item being classified. The significance of the modifier "Soviet" is not quite clear; does it mean Russian communism, and hence cover all communism in Russia, or does it mean that if communism in Russia were to lose the particular government by the Soviets (Councils) and employ more village (mir) meetings as instruments of government, classification would go differently?

Of course, these matters could not and should not be taken up in the swift course of a newspaper comment; the meaning of the sentence may be sufficiently clear to the reader for the purposes at hand. But the author should have these clarifying distinctions more or less available if he should be pressed. It is a clear and explicit frame of mind I am urging, not an extension of discourse. What is required is an analytical predigestion of the material to be expounded combined with felicity of phrase and economy of expression.

5. Verification and the Search for Truth

HAD he stayed for an answer, I am sure Pilate would have been in for an extended discussion. Even that portion of the discussion dealing with the relation of poetry to truth is formidable. Coleridge did not avoid the problem by saying that poetry is not concerned with truth, only with pleasure. Those who, like Wimsatt and Brooks, claim that poetry, far from being unconcerned with truth, contains in the "poetic principle" the only eternal truth, become involved in difficult problems of proof.[1] Tate, commenting on Coleridge, says, "Truth is only the secondary consideration of the poet, and from the point of view of positivism, the knowledge, or truth, that poetry gives us is immature and inadequate."[2] And, for different reasons, Richards comes out at the same place: "It is evident that the bulk of poetry consists of statements which only the very foolish would think of attempting to verify. They are not the kind of things which can be verified."[3] Wellek and Warren, seeking to shed some light into this thicket, suggest, first, that the question of truth in poetry is a semantic confusion and that in any event it is better to stick to the adjectival form, "true" rather than "truth." In the second place, they suggest the verification procedure is one of squaring the statements with one's own experience, that is, does the poetic statement "ring true?"[4]

The critic does not emerge from this discussion unscathed;

1. *Literary Criticism, A Short History,* p. x.
2. Allen Tate, *The Man of Letters in the Modern World,* p. 56.
3. *Principles of Literary Criticism,* p. 272.
4. *Theory of Literature,* p. 23.

he bears the marks of confusion between the truth or verification of the poetic phrases, with the truth or verification of his
own. We are, fortunately, concerned only with the critic's
statements which fall under the same standards of truth and
falsity, verification or lack of it, as any other prose statements
analyzing some portion of the empirical world. This does not
emancipate them from difficulties—they share with all statements employing evidence the problem of how one is to interpret the relation of sensory perception to external reality.
Critical propositions also must confront the question of causa-
tion; as Reichenbach shows, they must settle for a statistical
answer in terms of probability;[5] and as Lazarsfeld suggests,
they must be content with an experimental answer in terms of
an association that cannot be destroyed by any intervening
variable.[6] But these problems of truth and verification have
not seriously impeded other areas of analysis, and there is no
reason why they should do so here.

The relationship between generalized statements and statements about particulars is complex, for upon examination it
appears that every statement about some particular person or
event or poem relies upon a very large number of implicit
generalizations. The more interesting questions, however,
have to do with the way in which generalizations or "laws" or
hypotheses or principles may somehow or other be tested so
that we can find out if they are true, or to what extent they
are true. One way of doing that is to see if they may be subsumed under other more general hypotheses, invoking the
general rules of logic. If one does this properly, so that the
argument is *valid,* one may say that to the extent that the more
inclusive hypothesis, the major premise, is true, so also is the
lesser one. One trouble with this is that the more inclusive

5. Hans Reichenbach, "Probability Methods in Social Science," in Daniel
Lerner and Harold Lasswell, eds., *The Policy Sciences* (Stanford University
Press, 1951).

6. Paul Lazarsfeld, "Evidence and Inference in Social Research," in Daniel
Lerner, ed., *Evidence and Inference* (Glencoe, Ill., The Free Press, 1959).

hypothesis is likely to have a probability less than one, and hence inferences from probabilistic minor premises become increasingly risky. And, in any event, the problem of verifying the more inclusive hypothesis is, at every step, always present. Most propositional systems are not axiomatic anyway; each proposition must usually be referred to its own data in order to earn some truth-value.

So, sooner, rather than later, we come to the verification of empirical generalizations in literary criticism.[7] At the very beginning the difference between discovering these generalizations, uncovering the regularities that may reside in the poetic process, bringing probable causes for various effects to the light of day, are all very different from their testing and verification. It is confusion on this point that often sends the imaginative innovator into a state of shock about the usual verification procedures. Discovery and insight may come from a wholly subjective reference; testing and verification rarely if ever can be achieved in this way. But what are these usual verification procedures?

It is convenient to take as an example Kenneth Burke's statement about the relation of formal design to theme: "Whatever the theme may be . . . [formal designs, such as meter] add saliency to this theme, the same design serving to make dismalness more dismal or gladness gladder."[8] How would one test such a proposition? In the first place, one would have to develop an unambiguous, univocal, set of meanings for the terms employed. I am not sure that "formal design," "saliency" and therefore "adding saliency," and "theme" have such unequivocal meanings—but they could be assigned such meanings. In doing this, for purposes of verification, one would give them *operational* meanings, in Bridgman's sense,

7. It is important to notice here that the reference is to generalizations or universal statements; for a broader treatment of verification procedures see A. J. Ayer, *Language, Truth, and Logic* (New York, Dover Publications, 1952), pp. 15–16.

8. *Counter-Statement*, p. 135.

so that there would be clear explicit criteria to know when one was dealing with a "theme" for example, and not an "idea," "plot," or "image."

A word about such operationalism is in order because it is a treacherous business. It involves paring away meanings to leave a term in its stripped and objectively recognizable state. Nobody likes to throw away some of the subtlety of his statement, some of the nuances and shades which may distinguish it from a more prosaic and less interesting account, least of all literary people. Theoretically this is not necessary—one can express as many different meanings and shades as one likes, each with its own term imbedded in its own sentence, and each satisfactorily operationalized—but practically, of course, the operationalization of a term does tend to be reductionist. Tastes differ in these matters; some prefer more ambiguity and associative content in their terms, at the sacrifice of clarity and reliability in verification, others like things better the other way around. But one thing is clear: If it ever should make any difference whether a statement is true or not, that is, whether it could be verified by the usual procedures, some ambiguity would have to be sacrificed for clarity.

Sometimes a variable, like "formal design" or "theme," does not lend itself to verification procedures such that all aspects may be tested at once; it may be too massive, complex, intractable, remote, and so forth. Then one needs to establish an indicator which is thought to vary the way the whole variable would vary. In Burke's proposition he gives us a clue: he suggests that meter is a representative example of the various kinds of formal design. Thus we would be able to approximate a test of the larger relationship between formal design and theme by testing the relationship between meter and theme, a much easier matter. This is satisfactory if the indicator, meter, is a valid representative of the more inclusive quality, formal design. Burke did not say it was, he only said it was an example of what he meant, but the tests would cast light on the truth of the general proposition.

If both variables are now in shape for the test procedure, one must look at the nature of the relationship implied. It is stated as an invariant relationship, universal and categorical. This would mean that a single contrary instance would disprove it. But assuming it is meant as a probabilistic statement, with the phrase "tends to"[9] understood, we will interpret the proposition to mean that wherever there is a formal design there is likely to be increased saliency of theme. This then is a proposition about the probability of a frequency distribution.

Verification operations always involve comparisons; in this case one could compare two samples of literary statements with similar themes, one with a specified formal design, say meter, and the other without it. Comparing one with the other, one could judge, for oneself at least, whether the proposition is true, whether there is such a tendency as Burke alleges. Alternatively, since verification might employ the experimental as well as the observational method, one could try the same statements on one's sensibility with and without meter, to test whether or not the meter added saliency. Of course the whole testing procedure would be infinitely superior if one tried it on a group of people, selected on some systematic basis—but we shall come to this in a moment.

Finally, it is a matter of some importance whether or not the examples of literary work were picked in a biased fashion or in some more scientific fashion. It is illustrative, at this point, to see what Burke himself did to establish his proposition. In effect, he gave some illustrations, employing, not meter, but "talking at cross purposes" as his example of formal design. For these illustrative purposes, his sampling is as follows. He points out that "talking at cross purposes" can add saliency to a humorous effect in an instance he gives from ordinary life; it can do the same for "sournoiserie" as is demon-

9. See R. B. Braithwaite, *Scientific Explanation* (Cambridge University Press, Eng., 1955), pp. 361–66, for a discussion of "tendency statements."

strated in the scene from Wilde's *Salome* where Salome insists she will kiss Iokanaan on the mouth; it intensifies sentiment in Wordsworth's poem "We are Seven" and a sense of tragic irony in Racine's account of Agamemnon's deception of Iphigenia with respect to his plan to sacrifice her.[10] But his illustrations, revealing a sampling procedure criticized by others, do not verify the proposition that there is such a general relationship as he claims; they only establish that he can find instances where it does, or he thinks it does, hold true. Verification would have required a systematic random sampling of some specified literary population. Otherwise, of course, someone else could come along with a set of examples which tended to establish the contrary relationship. A demonstration that something *can* happen is not at all a verification of a statement that it *tends to* happen.

Who shall judge whether the formal design added saliency to the theme? In a sense Burke lets the reader judge for himself by presenting examples of what he is talking about, and even if his sampling of instances were better he still could let the readers judge, though it might be arduous. But the judgment in these cases involves an imaginary contrast with what the literary passage would be like if the formal design were absent—a notoriously difficult thing to do. Burke is asking each reader to do as he has done, but in this way the readers have been influenced to perceive what they have been told to perceive.[11] Moreover, all the advantages of independent outside observation or experiment are lost: there is no reporter for comparing the various experienced effects and bringing them together, there is no analyst, there is no way to compare the qualities of the readers to learn about the relation of reader quality to perception of added saliency—an

---

10. *Counter-Statement,* pp. 135–38.

11. There is a sense in which the critic is constantly engaged in a self-fulfilling prophecy. If a person reads Charles Feidelson's statement that one means whereby Poe creates an uncanny horror effect is through his ambiguous metaphysics, forever after this will be true for him.

important feature of literary effect. It is clear enough that only a truly observational or experimental research design will serve the purpose of verification, though I would hope that some experiments might be conducted with those whose sensibility is most developed—the critics themselves.[12]

There are, of course, tests to help us decide if the relationship is one that could easily have happened by chance. There are ways of holding constant some other factor (such as rhyme, if we were testing meter) to make sure that the inferences we are drawing from the relationship are the correct ones. There are many procedures of this nature to guide the verification process and the analysis which follows it. But I am sure it seems to many that this verification is too costly; it is too destructive of much that is fine and beautiful in the critical process, and perhaps this is so much the case that one should stop here and be content with the present state of the art. Three considerations argue against this. One is the possibility of reconciling persistent differences among critics. Another is that the single exploratory experiment with which I am familiar seems to have been enormously useful for the critical process itself. Hence other experiments, better designed and more modern in approach, seem desirable. The third is the possible influence upon students and citizens, of the example of an important branch of learning propounding hypotheses and principles without any effort ever to verify them. Each of these deserves a brief examination.

One of the recurring themes in the critical literature is the dissatisfaction with the variety of interpretative methods, literary canons, principles, and judgments. To take two examples, in the earlier discussion of literary theory, we showed how Richards, Pound, and Eliot each had a different theory of imagery, different propositions on what gave an image its

12. I am aware that something called cooperative criticism was attempted once at Columbia in 1941, without notable success. However eminent the critics on that occasion, the effort did not in any sense approximate a verification process for empirical generalizations in literary theory.

effectiveness.[13] Perhaps they are all true; perhaps they are true for different kinds of imagery; perhaps they are true for different kinds of people; perhaps they are all false. A second example is available in the contrasting statements on formal design such as meter in Burke's formulation above, and Richards' statement, based on his experimental work, to the effect that meter and verse form tend to "distract" many readers.[14] Are these compatible? When? How? For whom?

We have been talking about the verification of empirical generalizations, something different from the interpretation of individual works. But if the generalizations were better established, and the concepts better defined, and the theory more explicit, the interpretation of a particular work would benefit in clarity, plausibility, and capacity to convince a fractious fraternity of critics. It would be possible, then, to distinguish between those interpretations which are essentially of the form "Here is what *I* see in a work; can you follow me?" and those which are of the form "Here is what people with certain credentials must see in a work. Follow us." Consider, in this light, the following comment by Monroe Beardsley whose work does something to establish those "plausible principles" which he finds lacking in the instance he cites:

> It is hard to see what plausible principles would justify the method of explication used by Elder Olson, *The Poetry of Dylan Thomas*, Chicago: U. of Chicago, 1954; for example, he says that "And from the windy West came two-gunned Gabriel," refers to the constellation Perseus, for Perseus had two weapons, his sword and Medusa's head; two guns recall the Wild West, the West recalls poker, poker is a game of cards, cards suggest trumps, and trumps suggest the Last Trump, hence Gabriel (p. 74). Is there any limit to explication by this method?[15]

13. See above, p. 39.
14. *Practical Criticism*, p. 190.
15. *Aesthetics, Problems in the Philosophy of Criticism*, p. 158.

But if men disagree on the interpretation, how can such disagreement be resolved except by recourse to better and more "plausible" principles—principles made plausible by hard experimental research and other systematic processes. (In this case, of course, the problem is one of associative thinking on which there is already some relevant work.)

The exploratory experiment I have in mind, of course, is that of I. A. Richards. He did not set out to verify any propositions; it was an exploratory operation with rather loose hunches in mind, but the effect is, like any other verification, to build up the probability that certain relationships hold true for certain kinds of poems and certain kinds of people. Mr. Richards, starting out with the view that "the history of criticism . . . is a history of dogmatism rather than a history of research,"[16] gave to his students at Cambridge four poems a week over a period of years, asking them to review them carefully and to comment freely on them in writing. They were asked to return their comments at the end of a week's time, and to note the number of readings given to each poem. None of the students was told the authors of the poems or given more explicit instructions on the nature of the experiment. Although the size and exact composition of the sample is not clear, there were "several hundreds of opinions upon particular aspects of poetry" and this represents about a 60 per cent return from the students in Mr. Richards' classes, presumably from the more interested and informed members of the class.

The first set of findings has to do with the difficulties of interpretation. These include: difficulty in understanding the plain sense of poetry, difficulty in sensuous apprehension, variation in the capacity to interpret and use the poem's imagery, the intrusive effect of irrelevant and personal associations, the employment of stock responses, sentimentality, inhibition, doctrinal adhesions, and general critical and technical presuppositions.[17] This opens up a storehouse of im-

16. *Practical Criticism*, p. 8.
17. Ibid., pp. 189, 191, 196, 201.

portant ideas, some of which are further explored in the
detailed analysis of the experiment. Many propositions
emerge from this discussion, far too many to state here. To
illustrate (with slight paraphrasing):[18]

> Misunderstanding of the "plain sense" of the poem is a
> function of "grudges felt on other grounds" [perhaps
> ideological opposition or "doctrinal adhesions"].[19]

> Imaginative reality is an inverse function of mixed meta-
> phors "when such a fusion is invited that the several
> parts cancel one another."

> The dissipation of emotional impulses tends to be pre-
> vented by condensation and economy in poetry.

> Control of feelings is a function of control over thought.

These, and the other propositions which I have mentioned
in this discussion may seem too stripped, too bare, too much
like copy-book maxims. But it has been the experience of
other fields that simple straightforward propositions not very
different from these lead to fruitful research, fruitful new
hypotheses, fruitful differentiation of situations. Perhaps it is
the tradition of ambiguity which stands in the way; perhaps
it is a sense that ambiguity is a kind of "depth" of understanding which clarity dispels (and sometimes it is—but often it is
not); perhaps it is that age-old truth that everything seems
obvious, including its opposite, when we have entertained
several opposing views in our mind quite comfortably for

18. Ibid., pp. 13–17.

19. I cannot forbear to comment at this point on one of the fortunate results
of explicit formulation. It begins to be clear from (a) Mr. Tate's comments on
the ideological basis for Wilson and MacNeice's criticism of Yeats, (b) Burke's
explicit statement that ideology affects poetic response to form—as when a
religious statement at the end of a series spoils its repetitive effect, and (c)
Richards' comments on doctrinal adhesions, that variation in ideology causes
variation in poetic effect, including the incapacity to make out the plain sense
of a poem.

many years. On this matter we can do no better than quote Mr. Richards' own caution:

> Critical principles, in fact, need wary handling. They can never be a substitute for discernment though they may assist us to avoid unnecessary blunders. There has hardly ever been a critical rule, principle or maxim but for fools a will-o'-the-wisp.[20]

But the unfortunate truth of the matter is that Mr. Richards did not pursue his "experiment" far enough, and did not employ his findings to establish explicit propositions for further verification. He uses his material, quite properly in the first effort of its kind, so far as I know, to discover difficulties, insights, a few rules, and as he says, "morals." He did not test or verify these principles; he did not even state them in such a way that they might be tested. He did not establish controls in his "experiment"; he did not sort out the factors that are regularly associated with each misunderstanding or difficulty; we hardly know anything about the association of educational background, age, or field of interest, let alone anything more recondite (and probably more relevant) about those who made one kind of mistake rather than another. It is, in short, a fishing expedition, not an effort at verification in any real sense, and not an experiment with any proper kind of experimental design. Hyman says:

> Our ideal critic would investigate the whole problem of what the poem communicates, how and to whom, using every available source of information to find out what it was meant to communicate; and then every technique from introspection to the most *objective laboratory testing* to find out what it actually does communicate to differing individuals and groups at different times and under different circumstances.[21]

20. *Practical Criticism*, p. 12.
21. Stanley E. Hyman, *The Armed Vision*, p. 392 (italics mine).

But no one has done it. In spite of a certain restlessness in the field typified by Mr. Frye, no one has fulfilled the promise of Mr. Richards' pioneer work. Apparently this area of research is posted: "No trespassing."

One of the most foolish of mistakes is for a man with a little specialty to look around him at others doing different things and say to them, "Look! Why don't you do your jobs the way I do mine?" Another bit of foolishness is for a man to pursue his narrow course ignorant of the effects, or most likely denying these effects. How a person learns to study in his history class has an important effect on how a person handles Latin; and what is taught in Latin has an effect on how a person handles research materials, organization of thought, sticking to the subject, motivation and attitude, pride in achievement, dogmatism, and a host of other things. If education does not have this more generalizable quality, we have been sadly misled about the importance of our tasks as teachers.

What is it that the citizen learns in a discipline which slights systematic verification and even scoffs at it? Consider the man faced with a problem in which emotional predispositions are heavily engaged and the amount of information available to even well educated people is likely to be minimal: I mean the desegregation of Negro and white children in school. Here, for example, is part of an argument presented by an Emory alumnus on the segregation issue. He is asking for the closing of the public school:

> When you get down to it, the question as to just how much value post-grammar-school education is to the general public is an intriguing subject. Few if any people are ever called upon to cope with or otherwise interest themselves in problems which cannot be readily answered from what they learned in grammar school, or could easily have taught themselves from those rudiments. Only professions and trades require slightly higher mathemat-

ics, chemistry, biology, or even more *recherché* information. As for "broadening the mind," one has only to look at the Germans who, despite their being the best educated people in the world, have twice led us into world holocaust.[22]

It must be clear that education has failed here, and not merely in the values held and the goals cherished. It has failed in teaching the uses of evidence, the proper canons of inference, the examination and verification of implicit theories. It will be terribly easy to persuade such a man that he already knows enough facts, that the topic is unresearchable, that his "principles" have been established by the only way one really can establish such principles—by introspection; that experimental evidence, or partial evidence from surveys is "trivialization" of a problem, that his system of sampling is quite adequate for him to establish generalizable rules, that when he says "race," "freedom," or "states' rights," the boundaries of these terms are sufficiently clear so that any further definition merely spoils his discourse, that without inquiry he knows how other people feel (because they all feel as he does—the right way), that when he cited "evidence" to show that intelligence is inherited he doesn't need to bother with such mechanical details as "controlling for education, or family, environment, or demoralization." In short, he can borrow a way of knowing and a set of attitudes toward research which—in a wholly unintended way—seem to legitimize his predilections.

Let me be specific: I am talking about the verification of propositions, not about specific values, not about other kinds of research or the scholarly approach in general. I am saying that the failure to acknowledge, specify, and verify generalized thinking, and the failure to give status to the only possible means of doing these things, is dangerous and dysfunctional

22. Thomas J. Wesley, Jr., "Must We Integrate to Educate?" *The Emory Alumnus* (November 1959), p. 15.

for the citizen in the situation I have described. The subjectiv-
ist, self-referential, and occasionally autistic quality of
thought encouraged in literary criticism forms a Way of
Knowing. There are times when this epistemology, too well
learned, may stand in the way of an orderly and flexible society.

6. Evaluation and Due Process

I T is convenient," say Wellek and Warren, "to distinguish between the terms 'value' and 'evaluate,' "[1] and we shall find it convenient to distinguish between two aspects of evaluation. There is, in the first place, the process of arriving at a clear formulation of an individual's or a society's values, aesthetic, moral, even political. It is to this process which the critics refer, I think, when they speak of the study of literature as an "organization of experience." We shall return to this later. But there is another aspect of the term "evaluate" which is closer to judging and which consists primarily of deciding whether a particular case embodies the values arrived at by the other and earlier process, or is deficient in some respect. In the discussion I have read there is a tendency to confuse these two aspects of evaluation and hence to formulate the critic's problem in somewhat cloudy terms.

There is, I think, a general consensus that the tendency of the critics of the modern day has been to devote less attention to the judgmental function of the critic and rather more to the analytical. Wimsatt and Brooks report this with some re-gret,[2] Wellek and Warren with some skepticism that it can be done.[3] The clear separation of the two functions was sug-gested earlier in Richards' view that the theory of criticism was comprised of two parts, a theory of communication and a theory of evaluation. But this was for analytical purposes and

---

1. *Theory of Literature*, p. 227.
2. *Literary Criticism, A Short History*, p. 735.
3. *Theory of Literature*, p. 238.

in practice he did not separate them. Given the evident tendency of the times, the question of whether this is desirable or not—indeed, the whole matter of the proper function of the critic—is up for review. Brooks is quite explicit: "The Humanities are in their present plight largely because their teachers have more and more ceased to raise normative questions, have refrained from evaluation."[4] To which Mr. Frye replies: "Although it [the theory of literature] takes certain literary values for granted, as fully established by critical experience, it is not directly concerned with value-judgments."[5] An intermediate view, perhaps, is represented by what has been called the "Chicago Neo-Aristotelian" group, interested in the "grounds of criticism," that is, the method by which judgments are formulated—a concern which is immediate to our own interests.

The idea of a completely value-free analysis is a chimera and should be disposed of at the beginning. The important question is: At what point shall personal preferences and values be permitted to enter the analytical process? They inevitably affect (a) the decision of what to investigate, (b) the decision on the nature of the evidence to be allowed (revelation or scientific), and (c) the decision on what to do about the findings. They *may* enter at other points, but they need not, any more than logic need be corrupted by preference, correlations affected by desire, or statistical significance determined by wishes.

But we are concerned with a special kind of analysis: evaluation. It is no paradox to say that the evaluative process requires only two sets of values: (a) those that are established as the standard by which the work is to be judged, and (b) those that guide the procedure of judging. Of the latter, some preference for "objectivity," that is, public criteria, impartiality, adherence to the evidence logically relevant to the decision, "fair play," and giving the "defendant" the benefit of the

4. *The Well Wrought Urn*, p. 235.
5. *The Anatomy of Criticism*, p. 20.

doubt, where there is doubt, might serve as an initial guide. The formulation of the first set, the standards, is "substantive" and requires a critic to develop; our interests are procedural, because we are interested in ways of thinking.

The literature of criticism is scarcely devoid of canons for evaluative procedure. Yvor Winters, a critic who places great emphasis upon the evaluative component of his work, after outlining the preceding processes of research and analysis, describes evaluation as follows:

> the final act of judgment [is] a unique act, the general nature of which can be indicated, but which cannot be communicated precisely, since it consists in receiving from the poet his own final and unique judgment of his matter and in judging that judgment.[6]

The "purpose" of all other critical procedures "is to limit as narrowly as possible the region in which the final unique act is to occur." This procedure, of course, is limited to judging the poem against the judgment of the poet—and there are other ways of viewing this problem. In any event, since the act of judgment cannot be communicated precisely, and has not been communicated very generally, as a guide to procedure this statement is defective.

Richard McKeon adumbrates a more useful theory. He says:

> Evaluation may be achieved in general by comparing the effects of what is written on actual or chosen audiences or by measuring it against the canons for statements of the "kind" to which it belongs; the judges are either men conceived by various standards to be good and prudent or men judged to be expert in rhetoric or some other appropriate science of expression.[7]

6. *The Anatomy of Nonsense* (Norfolk, Conn., New Directions, 1943), p. 22.

7. "The Philosophic Bases of Art and Criticism," in Crane, ed., *Critics and Criticism*, p. 250.

This suggests two procedures, *either* of which will do: (1) comparing effects on audiences, (2) measuring the "poem" against certain relevant canons. This is somewhat obscure, because comparison is not necessarily evaluation; it becomes evaluation, however, when, as in McKeon's second procedure, a canon of some kind is brought along side for measurement. Let us try our own.

The process of evaluation, is, as McKeon said, a process of comparison, concluding in a classification. It is matching a work against a standard, and deciding whether or not the two are congruent. Thus it involves three steps:

I. A decision on a standard, or group of standards, appropriate for the work to be evaluated.
II. A decision on the features of the work appropriate for the standard (and establishing that the work has these features).
III. A decision on the congruence of the two.

The standards, of course, may be positive; for example some rough outlines of positive standards are indicated by the terms "multivalence," "imaginative integration of diverse material," "originality."[8] Or they may be negative: "shallow," "didactic," "florid." Now as a matter of classification, this process seems no different from that outlined above in Chapter 4, but the fact that we employ the terms "judge" and "evaluate" suggests a difference. The main difference is that because values are involved, special precautions have to be taken to prevent bias or irrelevance. Scientifically, perhaps, it is the same. Humanly it is different and the procedures employed should reflect this difference.

The term "judging" suggests a comparison with legal procedures employed in court, a comparison which may be useful for illuminating weaknesses in literary due process, something the critics are often very much aware of. But it would be the

8. But on "originality" see Monroe Beardsley, *Aesthetics, Problems in the Philosophy of Criticism,* pp. 490–91.

most arrant folly for me or anyone to suggest that the weaknesses are remediable in the same way the processes of law have
protected the rights of the accused. This is flatly a comparison,
not a prescription, a verdict, or a sentence. Due process in law
provides that each side of the case will have its own spokesman;
in a criminal trial, the prosecutor represents the state, the
counsel for the defense represents the accused. Due process in
a critical judgment has no such division of labor, unless it be
assumed that different critics will take different sides before
the bar of public opinion. This latter conception is false, however, because in the court the judge and jury necessarily hear
both sides, and hear them as they confront each other. In the
critical proceeding suggested, with different critics taking
different roles, different publics might hear different plead-
ings. So the critic must, in his own person, embody counsel
for both or all sides of the case; he must give all sides a fair
hearing.

Due process in a court of law requires that the jury and the
judge disclaim any special "interest" in the case; they must be
free to assess the evidence, and classify the result in terms unbiased by extraneous preferences. Due process in judging a
literary work can hardly have this protection. For one thing,
the critic may be a poet and therefore have a stake in critical
judgments. If not this, inevitably the critic will prefer one
genre or category of work, say the romantic poets, or certain
verse forms. If he is to qualify as a fair judge, however, he will,
I think, have either to set aside those preferences and judge
the work in the terms of its own genre, or he will have to shift
the grounds of the proceedings, call forth a new defendant,
declare a new trial and make this a trial of the entire genre.
He should not, in fairness to due critical process, confuse the
two.

Judges excuse themselves if they know a party at bar or have
relatives or friends or enemies involved in their decisions.
Jurymen are challenged in such cases. But the literary judge
moves in a milieu of colleagues, enemies, schools of thought,

factions, friends of the court (*amicus curiae* has a different
meaning here) and so forth. Some of the problems associated
with this situation are reflected in T. S. Eliot's comments on
the relations among critics.

> The critic, one would suppose, if he is to justify his exist-
> ence, should endeavour to discipline his personal cranks
> —tares to which we are all subject—and compose his
> differences with as many of his fellows as possible, in the
> common pursuit of true judgment. When we find that
> quite the contrary prevails, we begin to suspect that the
> critic owes his livelihood to the violence and extremity
> of his opposition to other critics.[9]

If judgment is a casualty of inter-critic warfare, surely something is wrong with the standards of evaluative procedure
which allow this to happen.

Due process in a court of law requires the law to be "no
respecter of persons." Justice is blind. But in the literary
courts there is a risk that the judgment of the works of an
author will be colored by his general reputation and will not
rest solely on his performance contrasted to the criteria previously established. If it were possible to judge a work without
knowing the name of the author, this problem of prejudice
would be avoided. This was in fact done once, as we have
noted, by I. A. Richards, in his experiment in *Practical Criticism,* where he offered anonymously to his students poems by
a variety of authors, including Christina Rossetti, John Donne,
George Meredith, Henry Wadsworth Longfellow, and also
including poets of no reputation at all, who were generally
thought to be merely "popular poets" of their day. The extended comments and analyses of these students prompted
Richards to comment:

---

9. "The Function of Criticism," in Irving Howe, ed., *Modern Literary Criticism,* p. 39.

How entirely a matter of authority the rank of famous poets, as it is accepted and recognized by public opinion, must be. Without the control of this rather mysterious, traditional authority, poets of the most established reputations would very quickly and surprisingly change their places in general approval.[10]

This leads him, and should lead everyone, to consider whether the process of evaluation of a work is not so heavily influenced by a pre-judgment involved in knowing the author's name and reputation as to vitiate much of its force. Only the strongest conscience reinforced by the strongest tradition of independence could mitigate, let alone overcome, this reputational problem.

Due process in a court of law has explicit rules on the evidence to be admitted. It must be relevant to the charge; it must be direct evidence (no hearsay); it must be material, that is, it should not be so trivial as to waste the court's time. The critic is not burdened by such formal rules. He is in fact apt to talk about the author's private life, his borrowings from someone else, his political views, his intentions—all in an effort to evaluate something quite irrelevant to these matters. F. O. Matthiessen was able to keep Eliot's politics out of court when he was judging him;[11] but Tate has charged that Edmund Wilson and Louis MacNeice were influenced by their dislike for Yeats' politics when they dismissed him as "romantic."[12] As for the material quality of the evidence, there is, I think, a tendency to extend the evaluative record to bring in anecdote and amusing story which may distract from the judging process. There is no provision to keep the literary court in order.

On more than one occasion the Supreme Court has declared

---

10. *Practical Criticism,* p. 315.

11. *The Achievement of T. S. Eliot* (New York, Oxford University Press, 1947).

12. *The Man of Letters in the Modern World,* p. 228.

a law unconstitutional because it was too vague; a man hardly
knew when he was transgressing. The literary court suffers
mightily from this difficulty. The very nature of the illustrations given in the outline of evaluative procedure suggests
some of the difficulty: "multivalence," "shallow," "florid"—
virtues and defects which are employed as criteria. Here, for
example, is a criticism of Theodore Dreiser, in an anthology
of American criticism. Stuart P. Sherman says of Dreiser:

> I have perhaps hinted here and elsewhere my suspicion
> that Mr. Dreiser . . . is not a great novelist, because,
> though living in a great society, he does not express or
> represent its human characteristics, but confines himself
> to an exhibition of the habits and traits of animals.[13]

Mr. Dreiser, it appears, later rehabilitates himself with a
statement about the "profound moral idealism" of the American people; but the point is that he is convicted on little more
than a failure to "express the human characteristics" of the
American people. Surely some concept of sharp criteria, clearly
expressed, well embedded in a discipline, would keep this out
of the anthologies. But there has been improvement in this
respect (in spite of Frye's ironic comments on demoting Shelley "on the ground that he is immature in technique and pro-
fundity of thought," and then promoting him again "on the
ground that his love of freedom speaks to the heart of modern
man").[14]

There is a cognate problem which is relevant to literary
evaluation. In courts of law a man may not be indicted for
one thing, tried for another, and condemned for a third. But
in literary evaluation a work may be accused of one defect
and, without a decision on this point, may be condemned for
another. More important is the possibility that, having been

---

13. "The National Genius" in Irving Babbitt and others, *Criticism in America, Its Function and Status*, p. 250.
14. *Anatomy of Criticism*, pp. 23–24.

found guilty in one respect—a respect which the critic regards as important—the author's other qualities are not given a fair hearing. It is as though a man found guilty of drunken driving were then, *ipso facto,* suspect of peddling dope and of adultery.

The analogy is clearly only a rough one; I would not care to press it. But it should bring to light the fact that delightful, entertaining, instructive as an evaluative essay may be, there are many ways in which procedural weaknesses may lead to a misclassification, an error in judgment, a wrong verdict.[15]

There are, of course, all kinds of critics and all kinds of criticism. I have illustrated my critique of evaluative method with comments and examples that illustrate the defects, not the way in which individual critics have overcome these obstacles and achieved a great perspective and objectivity about the works they judge. Nor would it be a matter of concern if a few members of the profession displayed lack of judgment, or indulged their spleen—so do we all. The problem is an institutional one: there are no explicit standards for evaluative procedure; there is no systematic training in judicial restraint; there is no regular way to give a critic a bad conscience when he is violating some well understood protocol of criticism. It is amazing how well the profession does without these. How much better would they do with them!

Some of the consequences of this situation follow naturally. On the margins of the field, and perhaps within it, there is a tendency to plain obscurantism, a denial that the grounds of judgment can ever be adequately expressed and therefore that the effort is worth making. Apparently book reviewers like Orville Prescott and J. Donald Adams, and what might be termed a "public critic," like Mark Van Doren, are of this persuasion. Van Doren, for example, relies upon the position, "We do not know that much about poetry, and we never

15. After writing the above I came across the following title: Irving Babbitt, "Impressionist versus Judicial Criticism," *PMLA, 21* (1906), 687–705. Incidentally, this was listed among the three best pieces on theory and criticism in the *PMLA 75th Anniversary Issue* (December 1958).

shall."[16] On the other side of the field, on the border of aesthetics, we find Theodore Greene stating "The unique character of the artistic quality of a work of art can only be immediately intuited, and though it can be exhibited and denoted,
it cannot be defined or even described."[17] The element of
truth in this is suggested by Richards' comment, "Subtle or
recondite experiences are for most men incommunicable and
indescribable . . . " And the proper posture toward this truth
is revealed in Richards' work as it draws back the curtain a
little way on this "incommunicable and indescribable."[18]
Evaluative standards and procedures need not be a private
matter; it is, indeed, the virtue of the Chicago group that they
sought to make ever more explicit the grounds of criticism.

A second consequence of the failure of a more explicit procedure for evaluation is the dead-end dilemma posed by con-
flicting opinion. Here, for example, is an evaluation of Dickens
in which Santayana says "I call his, the perfection of morals
for two reasons: that he put the distinction between good and
evil in the right place, and that he felt this distinction intense-
ly."[19] And then again, Edmund Wilson says: "Dickens, in his
moral confusion, was never completely to dramatize himself,
was not, even in his final phase, to succeed in coming quite
clear."[20] Regardless of the outcome of the argument on the
general relation between art and morals, moral confusion has
never been considered a credit to an author; certainly it is
incompatible with "perfection of morals." But, without explicit evidence, and an evaluating due process which protects
the analytical process involved from extraneous considerations
and permits a proper weighing of the evidence, there is hardly
any way of resolving such controversies. A court of appeals

16. Quoted in Hyman, *The Armed Vision*, pp. 20–21.
17. *The Arts and the Art of Criticism* (Princeton University Press, 1940),
p. 389.
18. *Principles of Literary Criticism*, p. 33.
19. "Dickens," in Irving Howe, ed., *Modern Literary Criticism*, p. 122.
20. "Dickens: The Two Scrooges," in *Eight Essays* (Doubleday Anchor Books,
1954), p. 90.

means only a third judgment, possibly no wiser than the others, and with no superior means of deciding the conflict.

A third consequence is the apparent license, or at least lack of effective restraint, offered eccentric and "wild" judgments. Every discipline has them; political science is graced with not a few, but the tradition of a discipline, reinforced by an adequate evaluative due process, should exercise a moderating influence. Here, I am not talking about freedom and indeed encouragement of the heterodox theory, or the apparently implausible proposition. Evaluation, as we have noted, is different, and the difference, and the possibility of eccentricity, is illustrated by some of the judgments of Yvor Winters. He writes of Robert Bridges that a number of his poems "will stand the most scrutinizing comparison with any of Shakespeare's sonnets," and he is "probably the most finished and original master of blank verse since Milton." Next on his list is T. Sturge Moore, whose poetry he says "has been equalled by not more than two or three living writers" and who is a greater poet than Yeats. Moreover, it appears that Robert Bridges' daughter, Mrs. Elizabeth Daryush, is "the finest British poet since T. Sturge Moore."[21] These, and other eccentric judgments, are often hardly supported by evidence and sometimes come, without argument, *ex cathedra*.

A fourth consequence is the prevalence of fads and literary movements with some exaggerated proportions. Every field has some, and when we are dealing with evaluation—indeed, with literary taste—it is important that it be flexible and meet the conditions of the times. But the swings seem overlarge, and, moreover, the assessment of the criticism of each period is made difficult by the vagueness of the criteria and the terms used. McKeon says: "The history of critical discussions could be written in terms of a small number of words, which with their connates and synonyms have moved back and forth from

---

21. *In Defense of Reason* (University of Denver Press–Alan Swallow, 1947), fn. pp. 104–05.

obscurity to prominence in the aesthetic vocabulary."[22] And Northrop Frye, more acerbic, says: "The various pretexts for minimizing the communicative power of certain writers, that they are obscure or obscene or nihilistic or reactionary or what not, generally turn out to be disguises for a feeling that the views of decorum held by the ascendant social or intellectual class ought to be either maintained or challenged."[23] A literary due process should be, insofar as it is practicable, a protection against some of the worst excesses of this kind.

According to Auden, one of the functions of a critic is to help readers to become their own critics.[24] This is very different from getting them to like "the best" art and literature or convincing them of the correctness of a certain critic's taste. It is different precisely in the difference between learning values and learning evaluation. By watching a superior sensibility in motion they may change their preferences, but they will not learn the due process of literary criticism, they will not understand the gravamen of the charge, the weight of the evidence, the discrimination between the opinion and the holding, or the nature of the record. In the study of public opinion, there is a relevant distinction sometimes made between education and propaganda. Education is a discourse in which the audience is led to follow the argument and so to understand the basis for the conclusion; propaganda is a discussion where it is not.

At this point we have returned to the problem of citizen education. The prevalent style of popular evaluative discussion today is, in Riesman's term, comparative consumption preferences: statements of what "I like" and what "I just can't stand." The evidence and argument, obscure to the individual, become lost to the discussion. But our concern is only indirectly with taste; it is more centrally concerned with public affairs.

---

22. "The Philosophic Bases of Art and Criticism," in Crane, ed., *Critics and Criticism*, p. 251.

23. *Anatomy of Criticism*, p. 23.

24. See above, p. 10.

I have before me two evaluations of trade unions by men who have been exposed to some sort of college education, though, in one case, a rather indirect research experience. They were asked, rather generally, "How do you feel about trade unions?"

Ferrera: Well, I don't particularly care for them—because I think most of them are communist inspired, for one thing. Most of the officers . . . I think are hoodlums. Basically their ideals to begin with were good, but it's gone the way of all flesh through the years. . . . They brought the people out of the sweatshops. But too much money is being made by individuals. They tend to sway or control huge blocks of votes. . . . My own experience with unions has been very small, but the different people I see in unions are really nothing but hoodlums. And I know whereof I speak—in fact, one of them right here in the city is now serving 360 days or so—and he is the lowest type of individual—former schoolmate of mine . . . I only speak from what I see here; perhaps the top isn't so bad —instead of being hoodlums, they are educated hoodlums.

Flynn: Gee, I don't know. . . . I could take the pro or con in this case. . . . They just developed out of a desperate need that the working man had. It may only be coincidence, but the normal standard of living has increased over the period that unions have been involved in labor problems. . . . But I can see very well management's problems and complaints. The place where I'm assigned at the present time has a shop union—no national affiliation, and one of the results is that they have to keep from 5 to 10 [extra] people on their payroll. Annually this group will present management with a packet—"Here's what we're looking for." Rarely do they say, "This is what we're offering." Management is on the defensive, and every union is attacking constantly. (pause) This is important, of course, to the worker—that he has representa-

tives looking for his interests, because management, certainly has representatives looking out for its interests . . .
[and so on, until] I do think that the general need for
unions far surpasses any arguments against having unions.

This is not literature; it is a far cry from the subject matter
of critical evaluation, and the level of education may be below
the visibility of those primarily concerned with critical procedures. Perhaps the distance is too great for the relevance to
be material. But on the supposition that when one teaches a
subject one teaches a way of thinking, a method of evaluation,
we may wonder whether in the study of literature we are doing
more to encourage the first kind of evaluation or the second
kind. Are we producing versions of Mr. Ferrera or of Mr.
Flynn?

7. Thought and Language

In the literature of criticism a distinction is often made between the thought processes of the poet and those of the scientist. The idea here is not just that they express themselves differently; their basic thought patterns are conceived as different. There is a partially parallel set of distinctions in psychological literature which is useful briefly to explore.

Jung develops such a distinction in his study "On the Two Kinds of Thinking," one of which is called "directed thinking" and the other "dreaming" or "fantasying."[1] Bleuler, with a more detailed and empirically-oriented discussion, makes substantially the same distinction between logical or realistic thinking and autistic thinking, the latter term derived from his observation of the thought processes of schizophrenics.[2] These, he says, reflect the same processes embodied in dreaming, daydreaming, and fantasy life in general with "no sharp borderline between autistic and ordinary thinking."[3] Autistic thinking, like Freud's dream work, is distinguished by the strong affective component; it reflects wishes, desires, and moods, molds repressed material to the needs of the thinker, is amoral and illogical, ignores time and place and realistic possibility, and dissociates stable concepts and rebuilds them to suit the thinker's needs. The poet employs this kind of

1. See C. G. Jung, *Psychology of the Unconscious* (New York, Dodd, Mead, 1927), Chapter I.

2. E. Bleuler, "Autistic Thinking" in David Rapaport, trans. and ed., *Organization and Pathology of Thought* (Columbia University Press, 1951), pp. 399–437.

3. Bleuler, p. 404.

thinking to an unusual degree but maintains a conscious connection with reality all the while.

Both Jung and Bleuler base their work on the distinction Freud made between the pleasure principle which governs emotional life, and the reality principle, which governs regnant cognitive processes.[4] Freud's views are significant because they show the relationship between the two types of thinking. Mental functioning in the service of the pleasure principle comes first in the development of the individual and therefore in some sense it is more basic. It is uncontrolled, expressive, cathartic, and impulsive. As the individual becomes aware of his environment, he develops increasing consciousness and then, in order to direct this dawning consciousness, he develops a capacity for attention. To store the products of attention, he develops a notational system for storing experiences in his memory. Finally, the individual must develop a capacity for "impartial passing of judgment, which had to decide whether a particular idea was true or false, that is, in agreement with reality or not."[5] At this point the individual, while still retaining his primary process pleasure principle under more or less control, has evolved a secondary "reality principle." Freud thought of the substitution of the reality principle as a means whereby the pleasure principle might be given a stable life framework within which to work. The relationship is a complicated one but without the reality principle fantasying takes the form in which Bleuler watched it operate, schizophrenia or some other break with reality. Without the capacity for some fantasy life, some associative thinking, some pure pleasure principle, a life becomes dull, drab, uncreative. Clearly the education one receives is significant for achieving strength in both areas.

Probably the university education of today, the education which molds the guardians of society, is more likely to neglect

---

4. "Formulations Regarding the Two Principles in Mental Functioning," in *Collected Papers, 4* (London, Hogarth Press, 1953), 13–21.

5. Freud, "Formulations," p. 16.

the life of the imagination than the processes of logic. If there is any place where the thesis of this book is weak, it is here. Certainly the study of literature contributes richly to this area of life; in a way, this is the meaning of the "sensibility" which critics prize. To take only one example, Empson's analysis of ambiguity seems to rely very heavily on fantasy and free association. But this is not the only place for fantasy; there is such a thing as scientific imagination, and, as C. Wright Mills has pointed out, sometimes one discovers *The Sociological Imagination* at work. The point to cling to is that fantasy, free association, imagination of the possible and contemplation of the impossible must be encouraged along with a strong sense of reality. One study, indeed, shows that it is only those with the strongest grip on reality who can feel free to let their imaginations roam and indulge in creativity. They know that they can "come back" when they choose.[6]

Fantasy without some strong supporting reality sense may then turn out to be defective in quality, or "useless" to the individual, or socially disadvantageous. While I know the underdevelopment of a reality sense is the lesser danger, the problem is worth exploring briefly. Ayer mentions one possibility in his discussion of metaphysics: misplaced fantasy without logical restraint. He denies that metaphysics is in any important respect like poetry in that it uses emotive language in order to achieve its effects. Poetic "nonsense," he says, has a designed purpose, but the metaphysician "lapses into it through being deceived by grammar, or through committing errors of reasoning," or by indulging in some "genuine mystical feeling." This kind of fantasy life, he believes, serves no useful purpose, and detracts from the serious work of philosophy.[7] I am not, myself, able to judge the merits of this case—but it serves as a caution against one kind of unreal fantasy.

Another, closer to the more usual problem of the citizen, is

6. Frank Barron, "Originality in Relation to Personality and Intellect," *Journal of Personality*, 25 (1957), 730–42.

7. A. J. Ayer, *Language, Truth, and Logic*, p. 45.

illustrated in the responses of two men to questions about the nature of freedom. Ferrera, whom we met earlier in connection with our discussion of evaluative procedures, has a vivid imagination, and among my interviewees, showed the most marked capacity for free association. Asked what the word "freedom" means to him, he says:

> What it makes me think of is a pastoral scene—I don't know why—being soothed by a nice balmy breeze—green pastures, and a girl and a boy romping through the fields. That's what freedom means to me.

I suggest that this implies getting away from the noises and troubles of the city and he answers:

> It would suggest to me a closeness to God. . . . There are times I say what the heck to my existence—rather that or crying—you're bombarded by so much pressures of the present day, pressures of business, pressures of actual day-to-day living, pressures of whether you are actually bringing your children up right. . . . I think the recluse has probably got something that quite a few people wish they could have.

I ask him if he thinks people have too much freedom and he says he never thought much about that. I ask him about the dangers of freedom, are there any groups that would take advantage of it? He answers:

> Well, I can't single them out, but I would say . . . the Communist probably would. For goodness sake—you try to have me give you a definition of Communism, I don't think I could—but, yet, I would have to answer your question there.

He discusses matters loosely, with freely associative answers, with difficulty in speaking precisely and with a horror of definition.

Contrast his answer to that of another interviewee, a man with a better education, it is true, and with a scientific orientation. Asked about the meaning of the word "freedom" he says:

> Freedom always implies, I think, implicitly anyway, responsibility. I can't imagine a society which can permit unlimited freedom to any of its members. With freedom an individual must take upon himself the responsibility of acting in a way which will not be unduly harmful to the fellow members of the society.

He then discusses the nature of limited freedom; he turns aside the question on any sense of constraint he might feel (it isn't a problem); he believes that people are generally sufficiently self-controlled so that removal of some restraints would not create a situation where any one group would get out of hand.

This is an illustration of one of the possibilities of fantasy life in politics, nothing more. Among fifteen men, Ferrera was most prone to this type of thinking; it led him astray. The problem for education, humanistic and scientific, is to encourage fantasy and directed thinking into some stable proportion—realizing that they are not antithetical, but that, as Freud said, the reality principle supports a fantasy life in a viable framework. And of the artist: "with his special gifts he moulds his fantasies into a new kind of reality and men concede them a justification as valuable reflections of actual life."[8]

In passing we may note that it is his position as a man who must be an interpreter of fantasy material but who is condemned himself to employ a form of directed thinking which makes the life of the critic so arduous. The angry artist will attack him, as Karl Shapiro did recently complaining that the "student is left cold" by criticism and damning it because it

8. Freud, "Formulations," p. 19.

is no longer an "art."[9] And the man with no sympathy for
the subject of the arts, the controlled imagination, and the
fantasy which they employ, will find some other excuse to
berate the critic. It is a lonely spot in this somewhat inartistic
world.

Supervision of Language

We go to school to literature to learn about language, and
the critics are our tutors. We learn what is good and what is
bad, elegant and vulgar, powerful and weak. We learn that,
in the end, the most important consideration is to have something to say. But while we are learning this we also learn that
this is not an unbiased study of all the ways in which language
can properly be used. It is selective and it is guided by special
preferences. One hardly needs to explore very far before he
discovers that almost everyone makes the distinction between
the language of literature and the language of science, sometimes without prejudice, often in terms that seem to regard
the scientists' language as a poor relative of the language of
the arts. William Wimsatt and Cleanth Brooks speak of it as
"deprived,"[10] Brooks, as "frozen,"[11] and Tate has this to say
about it:

> It is the duty of the man of letters to supervise the culture
> of language, to which the rest of culture is subordinate,
> and to warn us when our language is ceasing to forward
> the ends proper to man. The end of social man is com-
> munion in time through love, which is beyond time.[12]

There is a little of Thomas Wolfe here, but there doesn't
seem to be much room for scientific language, unless it should
contribute to "communion in time through love."

9. "What's the Matter with Poetry?" *New York Times Book Review* (December 13, 1959), p. 1.

10. *Literary Criticism, A Short History*, p. 702.

11. *The Well Wrought Urn*, p. 9.

12. *The Man of Letters in the Modern World*, p. 22.

René Wellek and Austin Warren give a fair picture of what is at stake in the selection of scientific or literary language.

> The ideal scientific language is purely "denotative": it aims at a one-to-one correspondence between sign and referent. The sign is completely arbitrary, hence can be replaced by equivalent signs. The sign is also transparent; that is, without drawing attention to itself, it directs us unequivocally to its referent.

> [Literary language] abounds in ambiguities; it is, like every other historical language, full of homonyms, arbitrary or irrational categories such as grammatical gender; it is permeated with historical accidents, memories, and associations. In a word, it is highly "connotative."[13]

There is a strong case to be made to the effect that often the terms themselves are identical; it is their uses and influences on the mind that are different. This I take to be the gist of Richards' argument on emotive and referential language[14] and it seems also to be Northrop's idea in his discussion of "concepts of intuition" and "concepts of postulation" attaching to the same word.[15] Our interest, however, lies not in this issue but in the influence of the critic's exclusive concern with the uses or terms of literary, as contrasted to scientific, language.[16]

13. *Theory of Literature,* p. 11.

14. I. A. Richards, *Principles of Literary Criticism,* p. 267.

15. "For example the word 'blue' is used both for the concept by intuition, which is the immediately sensed color presented by the painter and the concept of postulation, which is the number for an unobserved wave length in electro-magnetic theory postulated by the physicist." See F.S.C. Northrop, "The Functions and Future of Poetry," in *The Logic of the Sciences and the Humanities,* p. 172.

16. You can't satisfy everyone. Erich Fromm complains that our education does not pay enough attention to the language of dreams, myths, and symbols and suggests special language courses for these. *The Forgotten Language* (New York, Rinehart, 1951).

Now it would be absurd to hold the critic responsible for teaching composition, grammar, or syntax, or even rhetoric. He deals with these as elements of artistic production, but he is not a composition teacher. In a somewhat different way there is no particular reason why he should prepare men for understanding and using the language of science; his aim is understanding drama, poetry, fiction. Thus, we are not surprised that another separate literature on the "Linguistic Aspects of Science"[17] should develop, or even that a separate science of significative expression should have been devised under the name of "semiotics."[18] But the complete divorce between the study of language as literature and the study of language as a system of communication must impoverish each other, the more so because they often discuss the same kinds of things. For example, in Roger Brown's *Words and Things* (1958) there is a discussion of "reference and meaning," "phonetic symbolism and metaphor," "linguistic relativity," and other matters of interest to the student of literature. Among the 219 references in the back, I found the names of I. A. Richards and Allen Tate, but I looked in vain for mention of Cleanth Brooks, Van Wyck Brooks, Burke, Crane, Eliot, Frye, Stanley Hyman, Ransom, Trilling, Wellek, Edmund Wilson, Wimsatt, or Virginia Woolf. On the other hand, I have examined the index of Wellek and Warren for the names of Sapir, Paget, George Miller, Whorf, and Zipf; they are not there. These authors have, it is true, one reference to Charles Morris —in a footnote at the back of the book. But the supervision of the culture of language, in Allen Tate's phrase, must be interpreted as a partial supervision of an important, but still only partial, area of linguistic development, analysis, and usage.

Within this area there flourishes a highly specialized and

17. See Leonard Bloomfield, "Linguistic Aspects of Science," in *International Encyclopedia of Unified Science, 1,* No. 1 (1955), 215–77.
18. Charles W. Morris, "Foundations of the Theory of Signs," in ibid., pp. 77–137.

well developed analysis of certain kinds of linguistic devices. The special terminology of rhetoric, including, say, catachresis, oxymoron, metonym, is a clue to the development of important distinctions of several kinds. Sophistication about irony, tension, ambiguity, imagery is very great. But it is an open question whether equal attention has been given to definition and precision and control over the slippery meanings of plurisignative or multi-vocal words and phrases.

It is true that Coleridge took such an interest, arguing that when "two conceptions, perfectly distinct are confused under the same word," the thing to do is "to appropriate that word exclusively to one meaning, its synonyme, should there be one, to the other."[19] As noted above, Wellek and Warren argue for the discontinuance of the word "philology" on the grounds that it has become "vague" and "ambiguous."[20] Kenneth Burke has shown considerable interest in terminology, as expressed in his "Lexicon" and *Grammar,* and reflected in his comment that "some terminologies contain much richer modes of observation than others."[21] Allen Tate, feeling the need for a term that would include both the logical properties of extension and intension, lopped off the prefixes and devised the term "tension."[22] But in spite of this concern for terminology Elder Olson can argue that a term as central as "poetry" itself has been allowed to drift:

> Criticism had to find points of likeness among an accidental accumulation of things of diverse natures which had been called "poetry" because in accidental respects they resembled it; and likeness it found; but these were *accidental* likenesses, as one might expect under the circumstances.[23]

19. *Complete Works* (New York, 1884), *3, 202.*
20. *Theory of Literature,* p. 27.
21. *A Grammar of Motives,* p. 472.
22. *The Man of Letters in the Modern World,* pp. 64–77.
23. Elder Olson, "William Empson, Contemporary Criticism, and Poetic Diction," in Crane, ed., *Critics and Criticism,* p. 37.

This problem of the control over word meaning is not a matter merely for the encyclopedist or the staff of a dictionary. The users of a term must try to give it precise definition. Ayer says, "a well chosen definition will call our attention to analytic truths. And the framing of definitions which are useful and fruitful may well be regarded as a creative act."[24] Carl Hempel analyzes the differences between nominal definitions and "real definitions" showing that within the general idea of real definition, there are two kinds of analysis, one dealing with the "logical" or implicit meaning of the concept to be defined, the other dealing with the empirical properties of this concept. An explication will include both.[25] But the critic seems much more interested in the connotative values of words than their denotative values. As a consequence his language loses precision, sharpness, and definition, just where he most needs it.

Of course, this problem is not limited to the students of literature. How often have the behavioral scientists employed the term "power" in a variety of senses? Harold Lasswell and Abraham Kaplan say "power is participation in the making of decisions."[26] Surely when Lord Acton said "power tends to corrupt," he had something else in mind. Robert Lynd says that the oldest sense of power is "dominance," and more recent meanings include "authority" and "social control." He quoted Bertrand Russell as drawing an analogy "between power in human affairs and energy in physics."[27] Indeed it is true that "ambiguity is systemic" in the use of language and will persist, but to have the guardians of language focussing on its richness and making a virtue of its ambiguities comes hard.

If, by chance, a conscious effort to avoid some linguistic

24. *Language, Truth, and Logic,* p. 86.

25. "Fundamentals of Concept Formation in Empirical Science," *International Encyclopedia of Unified Science,* 2, No. 7 (1952), 2–14.

26. *Power and Society* (Yale University Press, 1950), p. 75.

27. "Power in American Society as Resource and Problem," in Arthur Kornhauser, ed., *Problems of Power in American Democracy* (Wayne State University Press, 1957), pp. 1, 2.

imbroglio leads a man to invent a term, or to hyphenate two words and give the marriage a new meaning, he is accused of jargon. Such words, precisely because they do not have ambiguity and can be given precise meaning, do not have the "richness" connotations and associations which criticism prefers. The man who, in his extremity, says "A social object is an actor, which may in turn be any given other individual actor (alter), the actor who is taken as a point of reference himself (ego), or a collectivity which is treated as a unit for purposes of the analysis of orientation"[28] will find that his efforts at precision are not likely to be appreciated by those who like their language emotive, swift, and rich in associations.

Precision and the control of meaning is a tricky business. Words lose their precision in many ways. One way is through the variety of associations and connotations that they evoke. Another is for a single word to have a variety of different meanings that may become confused in speech, even though each is clear and denotatively different. A third is for a term to change over time so that a historical discussion may become confused on whether the author uses the word in the original or in the modern sense. A fourth and somewhat different source of confusion is the use of a variety of words by different people to convey the same meaning. In a sense the student of literature and the man of letters must bear a special responsibility for eliminating these sources of confusion, or at least for setting an example for others to follow. In his review of Parrington, Trilling gives the following analysis of Parrington's use of the word "romance":

Romance is refusing to heed the counsels of experience (p. iii); it is ebullience (p. iv); it is utopianism (p. iv); it is individualism (p. vi); it is self-deception (p. 59)—"ro-

28. Talcott Parsons, *The Social System* (Glencoe, Ill., The Free Press, 1951), p. 4. But the relation between precise thinking and clear communication of meaning—an issue raised by this sentence—deserves greater consideration than Mr. Parsons seems to have given it.

mantic faith . . . in the beneficent processes of trade and industry" (as held, we inevitably ask, by the romantic Adam Smith?); it is the love of the picturesque (p. 49); it is the dislike of innovation (p. 50) but also the love of change (p. iv); it is the sentimental (p. 192); it is patriotism, and then it is cheap (p. 235). It may be used to denote what is not classical, but chiefly it means that which ignores reality (pp. ix, 136, 143, 147, and *passim*); it is not critical (pp. 225, 235), although in speaking of Cooper and Melville, Parrington admits that criticism can sometimes spring from romanticism.[29]

Of course the social scientist will be patronizingly amused by this fluidity of meaning, until he reflects, for example, on the uses of such terms as "freedom," "rights," and "liberalism" in his own vocabulary. Here is a brief account of the use of the term "liberal" in an introductory textbook for the social sciences.

Liberalism is "spiritual freedom of mankind with the ideal of free individual self-development and self expression" (p. 4); the position of the liberal is that of "maintaining the bases of society," (p. 7); at first economic liberalism was "synonymous with laissez-faire" but later it came to mean "equalizing opportunities and liberating individual abilities (pp. 9, 10); political liberalism now means the same thing as economic liberalism but it once meant breaking down autocratic controls (p. 10); political liberalism has stopped meaning laissez-faire and means government intervention in social and economic affairs— except for people who are called "status quo liberals" who are still of the laissez-faire variety (pp. 10, 15); liberalism connotes "left" which is "made up of people who wish to revise the existing conditions or to improve the

29. Lionel Trilling, *The Liberal Imagination* (Doubleday Anchor Books, 1953), pp. 17–18.

general welfare" (p. 14); liberalism means "collectivist" viewpoint now—except, of course, for the "status-quo liberals" who are individualists (p. 15); and finally, "The liberal position of today is not one of complete agreement and self-consistency" (p. 16).[30]

It would be a mistake to blame the authors for all or even much of this confusion: the word has lost any single meaning and, like "romanticism," is useful chiefly as an evocative emotive word, with rich connotations. Some of these are largely evaluative, a risk reflected in Hyman's comment "Sometimes, like Winters' 'moral,' Eliot's 'traditional' means no more than 'good,' that he likes the work."[31]

But, if it is discouraging to see the single word mean so many different things, it is almost as discouraging, and just as confusing, to have a variety of words mean the same thing. In his rather intemperate review of the affairs of the literary critics, Karl Shapiro, a poet who must have no special aversion to ambiguity and ironic or even paradoxical uses of language says:

> Such terms [as "academic"] are very silly but they are anything but meaningless. If we could bear in mind that "academic," "intellectual," "modern," and what T. S. Eliot calls "classical," all mean one and the same thing and all refer to a specific type of literature, then we might be able to understand the nature of this official literary movement.[32]

It is not that Shapiro objects to synonyms; I suppose they are a godsend to poets; he simply feels that this is a kind of secret synonymousness which, until it is explained, creates an un-

---

30. Verne S. Sweedlun and Golda Crawford, *Man in Society* (2 vols. New York, American Book Co., 1956), vol. 2.

31. Stanley Hyman, *The Armed Vision*, p. 55.

32. "What's the Matter with Poetry?" p. 1.

necessary confusion. Perhaps a similar glossary of synonyms would have helped clarify an apparent conflict of opinion in 1957, when the same situation was variously termed, "a temporary setback," a "recession," a "depression," and "a rolling readjustment."

Another example of the same kind of confusion is given by an unfriendly, but probably accurate, critic of Croce. He says:

> If you disregard critical trivialities and didactic accessories, the entire aesthetic system of Croce amounts merely to a hunt for pseudonyms of the word "art," and may indeed be stated briefly and accurately in this formula: art = intuition = expression = feeling = imagination = fancy = lyricism = beauty. And you must be careful not to take these words with the shadings and distinctions which they have in ordinary or scientific language. Not a bit of it. Every word is merely a different series of syllables signifying absolutely and completely the same thing.[33]

This is, as a matter of fact, not an uncommon way of speaking. In the lexicon of the *National Review*, Democratic = socialistic = liberal = soft-on-Russia = unChristian. Pre-emptive concern with some facets of language, seems to have prevented a serious approach to the problem of definition and linguistic precision among the students of literature. We all need correction on this matter; none of us is quite free even in scientific discourse of a sneaking use of emotive terms to carry the referential meaning, or of nominal definition when we should employ a more analytical one. But the literary critic and analyst is not better in this respect; indeed he is a little worse. It is now thirty-five years since I. A. Richards said, "Construction, Design, Form, Rhythm, Expression . . . are more often than not mere *vacua* in discourse, for which a theory of criticism should provide explainable substitutes."[34]

33. Giovanni Papini, *Four and Twenty Minds*, quoted in I. A. Richards, *Principles of Literary Criticism*, fn. 4, p. 255.
34. *Principles of Literary Criticism*, p. 20.

It will be recalled that in *The Meaning of Meaning,* Ogden and Richards established a triangular relationship between word, thought, and thing. They effectively demolished the idea of a direct relation between word and thing; all such relationships were mediated either by the thought of the speaker or by the thought of the hearer—or, in communication, by both. For many years now a tremendous amount of fruitful labor has gone into the analysis of the relationship between thought and word, between thinking and language. The popular view that thought precedes language, that one first has an idea and then selects the right words and phrases with which to express it, has come under some scrutiny; certainly it is not that simple. There is substantial evidence that there is a reverse influence, as well, evidence which comes both from the study of individuals who have been linguistically deprived as children, and from cultural comparisons. On the latter point Benjamin Lee Whorf represents an extreme relativist position: he holds that every language reflects a particular philosophy and directs with a strong hand the thoughts and beliefs of those to whom the language is native.[35] The degree to which this is true is hard to determine; that it is true in some degree seems well established.

If our language structures, modifies, and partly determines our thinking we should be concerned to examine the language that we are taught, the preferred vocabulary of the educated man, the man of letters, and the man of science.[36] The influence of language, of course, is not limited to the words available to express thoughts—as the availability of a word to express mother's brother's cousin may help in thinking about

35. B. L. Whorf, *Language, Thought, and Reality,* ed. John B. Carroll (New York, Wiley, 1956). For an interpretation and critique of this view see Roger Brown, *Words and Things* (Glencoe, Ill., The Free Press, 1958), pp. 229–63.

36. "Art envisaged as a mystic ineffable virtue . . . may easily be pernicious in its effects, through the habits of mind which as an idea, it fosters, and to which, as a mystery, it appeals." I. A. Richards, *Principles of Literary Criticism,* p. 18.

this relationship. The influence is also effected through the figures of a language, the metaphors, images, and symbols commonly employed. Unless one is uncommonly careful, the rhetorical use of some such metaphor or symbol in political discourse tends to structure the discourse in terms of the metaphor, disputants losing sight of the fact that they are, after all, dealing with a figure of speech and not reality. Myths, symbols, personifications, images all tend to become hypostasized and taken, not for an adornment of an argument, but for the heart of the argument itself.

Nothing could be more convincing on this point than a glance through the social contract literature, where an imaginative symbolic act, probably first conceived as a figurative way of illustrating the nature of popular consent, soon became discussed as though it were a legal document with attorneys on either side hammering out the best possible terms. The notion that at some time men were "free" and then, for one reason or another, brought about this social contract is a persistent myth, reflecting in Rousseau's version, a happy dawn of civilization. In the famous phrase, he says "Man is born free; and everywhere he is in chains." The discussion on the nature of consent took the figurative language of chains, birth, and an imagined state of nature rather too literally with what seem to me to be unfortunate consequences for the state of the argument on man's relation to government. It comes as a somewhat unpleasant surprise, therefore, to read in the 1952 Republican platform the following preamble:

> We maintain that man was not born to be ruled, but that he consented to be governed; and that the reasons that moved him thereto are few and simple. He has voluntarily submitted to government because, only by the establishment of just laws, and the power to enforce those laws, can an orderly life be maintained, full and equal opportunity for all be established, and the blessings of liberty be perpetuated.

The surprise is unpleasant not because the myth is evil—it is not—but because the argument it engenders is sterile. Even worse, myths that persist because of their moral content or because they "speak to man's condition" become, like this one, embedded in the cognitive belief system of a people and hence often beyond argument.

The symbolic nature of political discussion presents the same difficulty. The symbol of the lighthouse, the beacon, the light in the window for the wayfaring stranger, are traditional to the point of triteness, yet there is a curious power in Emma Lazarus' lines on the Statue of Liberty, ending, "I lift my lamp beside the golden door." It is only a step from there, however, to the conception of a political platform as a somewhat similar beacon: "to uphold as a beacon light for mankind everywhere, the inspiring American tradition of liberty, opportunity, and justice for all—that is the Republican platform" (1948). Charles Feidelson has taught us how to look for symbols in literature,[37] but there the purpose served is integral to literature itself; in politics, particularly in a political platform, symbolist thinking is likely to confuse both the symbolist and his reader. If it were true that Herbert Brownell or Thomas Dewey was in the least deceived by the notion that either Mr. Dewey or the platform bore the relation to some audience somewhere that a beacon bears, say, to a ship at sea, the symbol was a disservice to the cause. But the audience to which this was addressed may have seen it this way. People are in fact deceived by the rhetoric of a campaign: Who knows how many people voted for Franklin D. Roosevelt because in 1940 and 1944 they did not want to be in a stream without a horse under them, or voted for Mr. Hoover in 1928 because the idea of chicken in their stew pots seemed attractive?

Personification offers a particularly powerful source of eliciting support for a political idea by drawing upon the range of affections that may be associated with a familiar or well-loved

37. Charles Feidelson, Jr., *Symbolism and American Literature* (University of Chicago Press, Phoenix Books, 1959).

figure. It is a way to make abstract qualities concrete, to evoke responses to these abstractions as to a person. In one of its forms it takes the guise of metaphor and embraces Ruskin's pathetic fallacy—the investment of inanimate objects with human emotions. Elsewhere it may simply present poems and nations as people, thinking and doing the things that people do. Thus John Crowe Ransom: "It is highly probable that the poem considers an ethical situation, and there is no reason why it should repel this from its consideration."[38] Or, European literature "does not, at its best, consent to be merely comprehended. It refuses to be understood as a 'symptom' of its society."[39] So also: "Even before de Gaulle came to power, France had in principle entered the Common Market, and the President subsequently gave assurances that he would not go back on France's word."[40] These are more than convenient summary statements; they imply a view of reality which their paraphrase does not imply; they invoke sentiments which the cold sense does not give; they implant "meanings" in Richards sense, of tone, feeling, and intention which are unique to the choice of metaphor. And this is why they are so useful—and so dangerous.

But perhaps the greatest trap of all is the reified image, sometimes called stereotype, of some group, nation, or particularly, "the people." It is so familiar to us that we hardly discern the blunting of perception in "We the people of the United States . . . "; "The Republican Party believes that regular and adequate income . . . "; "America is deeply interested in . . . the liberty of independent peoples"; or even in the book titles: *The American Mind, Making of the Modern French Mind*. T. S. Eliot says of the poet "He must be aware that the mind of Europe—the mind of his own country . . . is a mind which changes, and that this change is a development

38. "Criticism as Pure Speculation" in Stauffer, ed., *The Intent of the Critic*, p. 103.

39. Trilling, *The Liberal Imagination*, p. 277.

40. Sal Tas, "De Gaulle Against NATO," *New Leader, 43* (January 4, 1960), 3.

which abandons nothing en route."[41] In this context it seems quite meaningful for Leonard Hall to say of the critics of President Eisenhower's State of the Union Message, "nobody likes the program except the people."[42] But all of this implies a collective judgment, a distribution of decisions approaching unity, an attention and awareness in many individual minds which is rarely present, in short, a uniformity and group interaction which is not there. But because of the phrases, we imagine it to be there, talk about it as though this agreement and discussion had occurred, and draw from the fiction fictitious conclusions.

The relationship of language to thought is not merely that of instrument to craftsman. If, as in Latin countries, the language of emotion is well developed, the figurative and symbolic components are rich and expressive, words and phrases are heavily connotative, a man seeking to express political thoughts precisely and neutrally will have difficulty; more likely, he will not know that there is "another way" to think, politically. It is in this respect that the guardianship of language by those who prefer rich, connotative, expressive, and evaluative terms raises questions of a fundamental order. Ambiguous terms lead to ambiguous thinking; value-laden terms make causal analysis difficult; preference for connotative language means the use of terms imbedded in famous literature— that is part of the source of their richness, but this very fact means a kind of tropism toward old ways of thinking, old controversies, old cycles of argument. The terms and devices are important: figures, symbols, myths, images are pegs to hang ideas on, pigeon holes to put them in, graves to bury them in.

41. Quoted in J. C. Ransom, *The New Criticism*, p. 150.
42. *Straight from the Shoulder* (January 1956), p. 2.

8. Some Human Values in the Study of Literature

THE study of literature—and more generally, the humanities—yields to the reader a beneficence of untold, much discussed, and little understood values. Richards speaks of this as the organization of experience, the sorting out of impulses and development of discrimination; Auden speaks of the organization of emotions; John Dewey speaks of "reconstructive doing," of the creative element of aesthetic experience.[1] Of course, every important psychic event organizes experience—as those familiar with the way Orson Welles' broadcast of *The War of the Worlds* organized the experience of those who fled in terror into the streets will recall.[2] A beneficial organization is implied.

Throughout this discussion we have been asking how literature communicates. What effects does it have on various readers and types of readers—the best as well as the average? We have asked for theory, organization, verification. Now we need the fruits of such study, for in order to talk sensibly about the beneficial values of literary study, we should know what the effects are first. There are many books on aesthetics with theories on this matter, but on examination it turns out that they are based upon four kinds of evidence: the introspection

1. Dewey, *Art as Experience* (New York, Putnam, Capricorn Books, 1958), pp. 53–54.
2. Hadley Cantril, Hazel Gaudet, and Herta Herzog, *The Invasion from Mars* (Princeton University Press, 1940).

of the author into the qualities of his own experience, the author's empathic sense of how this experience might or should affect others (particularly others like himself), the report of other authors on these two matters, the report of poets on how they and others feel about poetry. This is not negligible; the report of a sensitive man on his own experience is valuable and must be incorporated in any analysis as a useful piece of evidence. But it suffers from the usual deficiencies of introspection, selective perception, idiosyncratic notation, and lack of comparability of findings, inaccessibility of the unconscious, rationalization. Moreover it is structured in the terminology and ideology of an outdated, usually "homemade" psychology which, I think, today carries limited conviction. On the other hand, a more or less systematic search through the recent encyclopedias, anthologies, handbooks, and bibliographies of sociology, social psychology, anthropology, and psychiatry does not reveal much useful material in assessing the value of literature to the individual.[3] Perhaps the philosophers are right after all. In a somewhat speculative mood, guided by fragments of research, and eager for correction, I will briefly comment on some of the values in this "reconstitutive" experience which comes from literary study.

A converging approach is in order. In the broadest sense, we are talking about what literate people get from their literacy. In Richard Hoggart's study of *The Uses of Literacy,* he describes the situation of the least educated in the following terms.

> Their education is unlikely to have left them with any historical panorama or with any idea of a continuing tradition. . . . A great many people, though they may possess a considerable amount of disconnected information, have little idea of an historical or ideological pattern or process. . . . With little intellectual or cultural furniture,

3. See "A Brief Bibliographical Excursion into Social Science and the Value of Literature" at the end of this chapter, p. 121.

with little training in the testing of opposing views against reason and existing judgments, judgments are usually made according to the promptings of those group-apothegms which come first to mind. . . . Similarly, there can be little real sense of the future. . . . Such a mind is, I think, particularly accessible to the temptation to live in a constant present.[4]

Among other things, then, the study of literature gives a sense of tradition, provides an ideological framework which, in turn, gives a certain consistency to thought and confers on individual opinions a larger "meaning"; it provides an exercise in making judgments and a time perspective to life.

Hoggart's study suggests that education tends to *civilize* people. If we may draw this distinction, it also tends to *humanize* them. Stouffer found that "in *all* age groups the better educated tend to be more tolerant than the less educated."[5] They also are less likely to categorize people in terms of their weakness and their strength and are more likely to encourage a tolerant and permissive upbringing for children. They are more optimistic about the future, too, a factor which probably "permits" them to be more relaxed and generous with other people.[6] Authoritarianism studies, which bear some relation to Stouffer's questions, also show that education is likely to reduce authoritarian tendencies.[7]

If we take a somewhat closer look, not at education or literacy, but at what is called "bookishness," a preference for reading rather than mere exposure to it, we find in Murphy and Likert's study of a quarter of a century ago that this factor is

4. Richard Hoggart, *The Uses of Literacy* (1957) pp. 158–59, quoted in Seymour M. Lipset, "Democracy and Working Class Authoritarianism," *American Sociological Review*, 24 (1950), 493.

5. Samuel Stouffer, *Communism, Conformity, and Civil Liberties* (Garden City, N.Y., Doubleday, 1955), p. 91.

6. Stouffer, pp. 91–104.

7. See, for example, Robert E. Lane, "Political Personality and Electoral Choice," *American Political Science Review*, 49 (1955), 173–90.

one of the main ingredients of liberalism—at least as they conceived of liberalism.[8] Their concept of liberalism as a uni-dimensional and relatively undated set of attitudes does not survive, and the relation of liberalism to "information" and to "intelligence" which seemed so certain in the thirties has pretty well been worn away, but a central ingredient of their scale is a kind of concern for the underdog, an equalitarianism, and this, I think, continues to be a function of education and, probably, of bookishness.[9]

It is apparent that these inquiries barely touch the surface of the problem. We must ask in more intimate detail how the experience of reading Dante, Shakespeare, Dostoevsky, re-structures a man's emotions, perceptions, personality. Three distinctions must be kept in mind. First, these experiences, like almost every other kind of experience, will have different effects on different people. Studies of the effects of television on children show that while the isolated and withdrawn child and the normal child may both watch the same gruesome pro-grams, they use their material differently: the withdrawn child evolves an autistic and somewhat morbid fantasy life out of what he has seen; the normal child selects material to be used in his active and social play life. Or, again, when comparable audiences are presented with arguments for a course of action, one audience exposed to one side only, the other to two or more sides, the persuasiveness of the two techniques is seen to vary substantially with intelligence. The more intelligent are more likely to be persuaded by the argument which deals with opposing considerations, the less intelligent by the one-sided

8. Gardner Murphy and Rensis Likert, *Public Opinion and the Individual* (New York, Harper, 1938).

9. A reservation on this point might be registered here. Recently as chairman of a panel for the political sociology section of the American Sociological Asso-ciation meetings, a study passed through my hands showing not only that social science faculty members were more liberal than other faculty members when they selected their fields and started their careers but that they were also likely to become even more liberal than others during the course of their careers.

appeal.[10] One thing that vitiates most philosophical and critical discussion of value, then, is this failure to consider the wide range of values affected by the personality, intelligence, and experience of the various readers.[11]

A second preliminary matter is the time period considered. The effect of reading a poem is almost certain to be different at the time of reading it, and later when its effect, if any, has been assimilated into the main body of the ongoing experience of life. In the persuasion studies the so-called sleeper effect has demonstrated how very deceiving about long-run influence a measurement immediately after an experience may be.[12] For the sake of precision, then, we would need to divide what is called "the aesthetic experience" into a short-term "aesthetic effect" and a longer term and more enduring "aesthetic organization."

A third distinction, too obvious to mention except for the tendency to speak of "the aesthetic experience" as a homogeneous concept, is the difference between reading Dickens and T. S. Eliot, Homer and Faulkner. The nature of the work makes a difference.

An outline for analysis of the values of the study of literature, then, allowing implicitly for these distinctions, would go something like this. In the first place I would suggest a kind of *placing* function, that is, the placing of the individual in a broader and more complicated world, with a greater variety of cultures, people, experiences than he might otherwise dream of. This, in turn, would be composed of two parts: (a) orientation, which might be understood to mean a picture of the variety of life, and (b) perspective, that is, an understanding of where a person fitted into this situation, combin-

10. Carl Hovland and others, *Experiments on Mass Communication* (Princeton University Press, 1949), pp. 201–27.

11. A fine piece of analysis on "Literary Experience and Personality" by Robert Wilson may be found in *Journal of Aesthetics and Art Criticism, 15* (1956), 47–57. See also Paul Goodman, *The Structure of Literature* (Chicago University Press, 1954).

12. Hovland, *Experiments on Mass Communication*, pp. 182–200.

ing, thus both cultural perspective and individual perspective. I take this to be the heart of W. H. Auden's comments on how the critic can help the reader. He says:

> First, he must show the individual that though he is unique he has also much in common with all other individuals, that each life is, to use a chemical metaphor, an isomorph of a general human life . . . for example, the coal miner in Pennsylvania can learn to see himself in terms of the world of Ronald Firbank, and an Anglican bishop find in *The Grapes of Wrath* a parable of his diocesan problems. And secondly the critic must attempt to spread a knowledge of past cultures so that his audience may be as aware of them as the artist himself.[13]

Such a perspective on oneself leads through a process of self-discovery to an understanding of one's own *identity*. There is considerable discussion these days of the problem of identity; it is an important emphasis for our time. Identity means a knowledge of "who" you are; such knowledge gives a sure sense of self, an awareness of what is ego-syntonic to one's nature, an avoidance of "phoniness," false fronts, poses, expression of unexperienced emotion, capacity to judge one's own skills and talents—in short, a reality sense and consciousness about oneself. One learns about oneself partly through comparison with other people.[14] I would argue that the "other people" of literature serve this function, and that the constant vicarious living of the literary experience gives one a basis for a rich and meaningful comparison. The more complex, deep, and true the portrayal of characters in drama and fiction, the more one learns through identification and contrast about oneself.

13. "Criticism in a Mass Society," in Stauffer, ed., *The Intent of the Critic*, p. 132.

14. See George Herbert Mead, "The Problem of Society—How We Become Selves" in Anselm Strauss, ed., *The Social Psychology of George Herbert Mead* (Chicago University Press, Phoenix Books, 1956), pp. 17–42.

Two facets of this aspect of the literary process have special significance for our time. One, a reservation on the point I have just made, is the phenomenon of pseudo-thinking, pseudo-feeling, and pseudo-willing, which Fromm discussed in *The Escape from Freedom*. In essence this involves grounding one's thought and emotion in the values and experience of others, rather than in one's own values and experience. There is a risk that instead of teaching a person how to be himself, reading fiction and drama may teach him how to be somebody else. Clearly what the person brings to the reading is important. Moreover, if the critic instructs his audience in *what* to see in a work, he is contributing to this pseudo-thinking; if he instructs them in *how* to evaluate a work, he is helping them to achieve their own identity.

The second timely part of this sketch of literature and the search for identity has to do with the difference between good and enduring literary works and the ephemeral mass culture products of today. In the range and variety of characters who, in their literary lives, get along all right with life styles one never imagined possible, there is an implicit lesson in differentiation. The reader, observing this process, might ask "why not be different?" and find in the answer a license to be a variant of the human species. The observer of television or other products for a mass audience has only a permit to be, like the models he sees, even more like everybody else. And this, I think, holds for values as well as life styles. One would need to test this proposition carefully; after all, the large (and probably unreliable) *Reader's Digest* literature on the "most unforgettable character I ever met" deals with village grocers, country doctors, favorite if illiterate aunts, and so forth. Scientists often turn out to be idiosyncratic, too. But still, the proposition is worth examination.

It is possible that the study of literature affects the conscience, the morality, the sensitivity to some code of "right" and "wrong." I do not know that this is true; both Flügel and Ranyard West deal with the development and nature of conscience, as do such theologians as Niebuhr and Buber.[15] It forms the core of many, perhaps most, problems of psychotherapy. I am not aware of great attention by any of these authors or by the psychotherapeutic profession to the role of literary study in the development of conscience—most of their attention is to a pre-literate period of life, or, for the theologians of course, to the influence of religion.

Still, it would be surprising if what one reads did not contribute to one's ideas of right and wrong; certainly the awakened alarm over the comic books and the continuous concern over prurient literature indicate some peripheral aspects of this influence. Probably the most important thing to focus on is not the development of conscience, which may well be almost beyond the reach of literature, but the contents of conscience, the code which is imparted to the developed or immature conscience available. This is in large part a code of behavior and a glossary of values: what is it that people do and should do and how one should regard it. In a small way this is illustrated by the nineteenth-century novelist who argued for the powerful influence of literature as a teacher of society and who illustrated this with the way a girl learned to meet her lover, how to behave, how to think about this new experience, how to exercise restraint.[16]

Literature may be said to give people a sense of purpose, dedication, mission, significance. This, no doubt, is part of what Gilbert Seldes implies when he says of the arts, "They give form and meaning to life which might otherwise seem shapeless and without sense."[17] Men seem almost universally to want a sense of function, that is, a feeling that their existence makes a difference to someone, living or unborn, close

15. John C. Flügel, *Man, Morals and Society, A Psychoanalytic Study* (New York, International Universities Press, 1945); Ranyard West, *Conscience in Society* (London, Methuen, 1942); Martin Buber, "Guilt and Guilt Feelings," *Psychiatry, 20* (1957).

16. Quoted in I. A. Richards, *Principles of Literary Criticism.*

17. "The People and the Arts," in Bernard Rosenberg and David M. White, eds., *Mass Culture* (Glencoe, Ill., The Free Press, 1957), p. 75.

and immediate or generalized.[18] Feeling useless seems generally to be an unpleasant sensation. A need so deeply planted, asking for direction, so to speak, is likely to be gratified by the vivid examples and heroic proportions of literature. The terms "renewal" and "refreshed," which often come up in aesthetic discussion, seem partly to derive their import from the "renewal" of purpose and a "refreshed" sense of significance a person may receive from poetry, drama, and fiction. The notion of "inspiration" is somehow cognate to this feeling. How literature does this, or for whom, is certainly not clear, but the content, form, and language of the "message," as well as the source, would all play differentiated parts in giving and molding a sense of purpose.

One of the most salient features of literary value has been deemed to be its influence upon and organization of emotion. Let us differentiate a few of these ideas. The Aristotelian notion of catharsis, the purging of emotion, is a persistent and viable one. The idea here is one of *discharge* but this must stand in opposition to a second view, Plato's notion of the *arousal* of emotion. A third idea is that artistic literature serves to *reduce emotional conflicts,* giving a sense of serenity and calm to individuals. This is given some expression in Beardsley's notion of harmony and the resolution of indecision.[19] A fourth view is the transformation of emotion, as in Housman's fine phrase on the arts: they "transform and beautify our inner nature."[20] It is possible that the idea of *enrichment* of emotion is a fifth idea. F.S.C. Northrop, in his discussion of the "Functions and Future of Poetry," suggests this:

18. William E. Hocking says this sense of purpose is conveyed to an entire nation through its art: "And whatever a nation accepts as giving valid and effective expression to its feeling—its song, dance, poetry, graphic art, architecture—in that, it avows something beyond its ideology but wholly pertinent thereto, namely, the quality of its purpose, its dream-of-worth, pointing beyond what it is toward what it aspires to be." *Strength of Men and Nations*, p. 26.

19. *Aesthetics, Problems in the Philosophy of Criticism*, p. 574.

20. Quoted by Edmund Wilson in his essay on "A. E. Housman" in his *Eight Essays*, p. 115.

One of the things which makes our lives drab and empty and which leaves us, at the end of the day, fatigued and deflated spiritually is the pressure of the taxing, practical, utilitarian concern of common-sense objects. If art is to release us from these postulated things [things we must think symbolically about] and bring us back to the ineffable beauty and richness of the aesthetic component of reality in its immediacy, it must sever its connection with these common sense entities.[21]

I take the central meaning here to be the contrast between the drab empty quality of life without literature and a life enriched by it. Richards' view of the aesthetic experience might constitute a sixth variety: for him it constitutes, in part, the *organization of impulses*.[22]

A sketch of the emotional value of the study of literature would have to take account of all of these. But there is one in particular which, it seems to me, deserves special attention. In the wide range of experiences common to our earth-bound race none is more difficult to manage, more troublesome, and more enduring in its effects than the control of love and hate. The study of literature contributes to this control in a curious way. William Wimsatt and Cleanth Brooks, it seems to me, have a penetrating insight into the way in which this control is effected:

For if we say poetry is to talk of beauty and love (and yet not aim at exciting erotic emotion or even an emotion of Platonic esteem) and if it is to talk of anger and murder (and yet not aim at arousing anger and indignation)— then it may be that the poetic way of dealing with these emotions will not be any kind of intensification, compounding, or magnification, or any direct assault upon the affections at all. Something indirect, mixed, reconciling, tensional might well be the strategem, the devious tech-

21. *The Logic of the Sciences and the Humanities*, p. 179.
22. *Principles of Literary Criticism*, pp. 44-57.

nique by which a poet indulged in all kinds of talk about love and anger and even in something like "expressions" of these emotions, without aiming at their incitement or even uttering anything that essentially involves their incitement.[23]

The rehearsal through literature of emotional life under controlled conditions may be a most valuable human experience. Here I do not mean catharsis, the discharge of emotion. I mean something more like Freud's concept of the utility of "play" to a small child: he plays "house" or "doctor" or "fireman" as a way of mastering slightly frightening experiences, reliving them imaginatively until they are under control.

There is a second feature of the influences of literature, good literature, on emotional life which may have some special value for our time. In B. M. Spinley's portrayal of the underprivileged and undereducated youth of London, a salient finding was the inability to postpone gratification, a need to satisfy impulses immediately without the pleasure of anticipation or of savoring the experience.[24] Perhaps it is only an analogy, but one of the most obvious differences between cheap fiction and fiction of an enduring quality is the development of a theme or story with leisure and anticipation. Anyone who has watched children develop a taste for literature will understand what I mean. It is at least possible that the capacity to postpone gratification is developed as well as expressed in a continuous and guided exposure to great literature.

In any inquiry into the way in which great literature affects the emotions, particularly with respect to the sense of harmony, or relief of tension, or sense of "a transformed inner nature" which may occur, a most careful exploration of the particular feature of the experience which produces the effect would be required. In the calm which follows the reading of

23. *Literary Criticism, A Short History*, p. 741.

24. *The Deprived and the Privileged* (London, Routledge & Kegan Paul, 1953), p. 84.

a poem, for example, is the effect produced by the enforced quiet, by the musical quality of words and rhythm, by the sentiments or sense of the poem, by the associations with earlier readings, if it is familiar, by the boost to the self-esteem for the semi-literate, by the diversion of attention, by the sense of security in a legitimized withdrawal, by a kind license for some variety of fantasy life regarded as forbidden, or by half-conscious ideas about the magical power of words? These are, if the research is done with subtlety and skill, researchable topics, but the research is missing.

One of the most frequent views of the value of literature is the education of sensibility that it is thought to provide. Sensibility is a vague word, covering an area of meaning rather than any precise talent, quality, or skill. Among other things it means perception, discrimination, sensitivity to subtle differences. Both the extent to which this is true and the limits of the field of perceptual skill involved should be acknowledged. Its truth is illustrated by the skill, sensitivity, and general expertise of the English professor with whom one attends the theatre. The limits are suggested by an imaginary experiment: contrast the perceptual skill of English professors with that of their colleagues in discriminating among motor cars, political candidates, or female beauty. Along these lines, the particular point that sensitivity in literature leads to sensitivity in human relations would require more proof than I have seen. In a symposium and general exploration of the field of *Person Perception and Interpersonal Behavior* the discussion does not touch upon this aspect of the subject, with one possible exception; Solomon Asch shows the transcultural stability of metaphors based on sensation (hot, sweet, bitter, etc.) dealing with personal qualities of human beings and events.[25] But to go from here to the belief that those more sensitive to metaphor

<hr>

25. "The Metaphor: A Psychological Inquiry," pp. 86–94 in *Person Perception and Interpersonal Behavior,* ed. Renato Tagiuri and Luigi Petrullo (Stanford University Press, 1958).

and language will also be more sensitive to personal differences is too great an inferential leap.

I would say, too, that the study of literature tends to give a person what I shall call *depth*. I use this term to mean three things: a search for the human significance of an event or state of affairs, a tendency to look at wholes rather than parts, and a tendency to respond to these events and wholes with feeling. It is the obverse of triviality, shallowness, emotional anaesthesia. I think these attributes cluster, but I have no evidence. In fact, I can only say this seems to me to follow from a wide, continuous, and properly guided exposure to literary art. Like so much else in this discussion, it is researchable, but so far as I know has not been researched.

Finally, we turn to a value which will have markedly different valences for different people: the maintenance of myth and illusion. "Without his myths," says Richards, "man is only a cruel animal without a soul."[26] O'Neill said as much about dreams and illusions in *The Iceman Cometh*. The matter is closely tied in with religion and the view one takes of the Bible, the Koran, the Talmud, and other writings of this nature.[27] It is, in my own case, reflected in a sense of loss that the cliffs, coves, and fields of the New Haven area (with a few exceptions) do not have stories told about them, are legend-free, do not have Gods and heroes, or even ghosts and pirates, associated with their names and features. But the moment I came to Hannibal, Missouri, I felt it; and I felt it playing on the Brandywine as a boy. A study of literature can do this; it can make history sing, and find books in the running brooks, and, if not good, at least a kind of human meaning in everything.

26. *The Philosophy of Rhetoric* (New York, Oxford University Press, 1936), p. 172.

27. "If the New Testament . . . had been written by a modern social scientist in the jargon of his profession, it would have died at birth, and Mithraism, or Manichaenism, or Mohammedanism would have taken possession of the European mind." Henry A. Murray, "A Mythology for Grownups," *Saturday Review* (January 23, 1960), p. 12.

There are certain things claimed for literary study which seem to me unlikely: I doubt if it produces kindness or empathy. Work on an empathy scale seems to have run into trouble,[28] but even if it were a valid instrument, I doubt if it would show much relation between empathy and the study of literature. (The emotionality of "depth" need not be empathy or kindness.) I doubt, too, whether the study of poetry, or fiction, or drama makes people more democratic, or *per se,* induces any particular political or personal ideology. The "bookishness" that I said earlier was associated with liberalism included history, religion, sociology, travel—everything. A particular social outlook is probably a function of a particular range of reading.

And there is probably a negative side. One of these is the one I have stressed—a tendency to misunderstand the role and proper function of figurative and emotive language, imaginative discourse, the collapse of logical categories, the nature and uses of verification. All of this, and more, I have included in my concept of mental clarity. A second risk is the danger of withdrawal from real life into a substitute, vicarious, or even fantasy life. Rudolph Arnheim suggests that this is the case with the "daytime serial";[29] Paul F. Lazarsfeld and Robert K. Merton have argued that the mass media represent a substitute for social and political participation.[30] I am dubious of the extent to which this is true but it may be more applicable to the study of literature. A third risk lies in the confusion of the nature of authoritative statement: one comes to respect and love the authors of the literature one loves and then to extend their sphere of competence to politics, public opinion,

---

28. A. H. Hastorf, I. E. Bender, and D. J. Weintraub, "The Influence of Response Patterns on the 'Refined Empathy Score,'" *Journal of Abnormal and Social Psychology, 51* (1955), 341–43.

29. "The World of the Daytime Serial," in Paul F. Lazarsfeld and Frank Stanton, eds., *Radio Research, 1942–43* (New York, Duell, Sloane, and Pearce, 1944), pp. 507–48.

30. "Mass Communication, Popular Taste and Organized Social Action," in Lyman Bryson, ed., *The Communication of Ideas,* pp. 95–118.

social maladjustment, an interpretation of "the times." This "halo effect" is a problem with all authoritative figures, but the nature of the attachment to well-loved authors (and their tendency to express themselves boldly) serves to intensify the problem in their case.

In all of this the critic serves as guide and counselor. But he must guide and counsel and interpret and evaluate in the language of the analyst, if he is not, while guiding through this wonderland, to teach habits of thought, speech, and mystery which take away from the value of his services and lead men and boys astray. This is not an impossible task. We will in the concluding chapter, consider in the broadest terms, the conditions of an effective union among the various disciplines: the conditions of a good education.

A Brief Bibliographical Excursion into Social Science and the Value of Literature

ANTHROPOLOGY is a logical first place to look because of its traditional interest in art and language. Fortunately there is an excellent encyclopedia in this field, *Anthropology Today*, edited by A. L. Kroeber (Chicago, 1953), but as we sample the articles on language, "The Relations of Anthropology to the Social Sciences and Humanities," history of cultures, folklore, it appears that we shall not find the answer here. The sociologists have a handbook, not quite so good, but only two years old and adequate to our purposes: *Sociology Today*, edited by Robert K. Merton, Leonard Broom, and Leonard S. Cottrell, Jr. (New York, 1959). There is, fortunately, an article on "The Sociology of Art" by James Barnett. On the first page we find the disarming sentence, "The sociology of art is comparatively new and its achievements to date are modest" (197). The selected bibliography contains 35 references; the discussion, as might be expected, deals largely with the relation of art to society, the role of the artist, the reflection of cultural values, the way in which art reflects cultural change. Most of the art under review is plastic art or music. The two-volume *Handbook of Social Psychology* edited by Gardner Lindzey (Cambridge, Mass., 1954), perhaps the best of the group, has no reference to literature, poetry, drama, or fiction in the index. There are two references to "art." One leads to an excellent discussion by Clyde Kluckhohn of Indian drawings as a reflection of unconscious processes. The other has to do with the relation of humor and laughter to art. *The American Handbook of Psychiatry* edited by Silvano Arieti (New York, 1959) has nothing in the table of contents to reveal an interest in art or literature, and no reference to literature, poetry, or art in the index. We come then to David Rapaport's *Organization and Pathology of Thought* (New York, 1951) for clues that we have employed where relevant. I have sampled the literature abstracted in the "Aesthetics" section of recent *Psychological Abstracts* and the section in *Sociological Abstracts* dealing with the "Sociology of Language, Literature, and Art." Some references to the contents of these sections are included in the next chapter. For the most part, they deal with psychological effects and social themes—not values.

9. A Humane Education in the Modern Age

THERE is something radically wrong at the heart of things. How is it that universities can so order their affairs as to slight the very essence of their function: imparting an understanding of how to understand, explaining the nature of explanation, showing how to weigh, test, verify the knowledge that we think we know? Surely the better part of wisdom is in knowing how to be wise.

The crux of the problem, I think, lies in the doctrine that there are "two worlds of truth" and "two methods of investigation" and that a chasm exists between the sciences and the humanities. Hence the crux of the solution lies in the knowledge that this is not so; that there is not, in particular, any formal difference between the humanities and the sciences in the appropriate method of theory formation, conceptualization, classification, verification, and evaluation—although the substantive differences will modify research strategies and the availability of proof will vary considerably. However one looks at it, there are not, in any event, *two* sets of methods. Perhaps it could be said there is a wide variety of analytical methods and schemes, but there is only one logic (with different notations) that gives to each of these schemes its rationale.

The history of this concept of a divided world has, of course, sources in the distant past and roots in the conflict between science and religion, but it becomes aggravated in the modern period, about 300 years ago, when science began to assume a

more "threatening" character. The comity of science and philosophy and poetry was disturbed in the seventeenth century,
at least in England, when the Royal Society became a visible
and distressing focus for scientific inquiry. Samuel Butler, for
example, writing "On the Royal Society," said:

> These were their learned speculations
> And all their constant occupations:
> To measure wind and weigh the air
> And turn a Circle to a Square . . .
> If Chymists from a Rose's ashes
> Can raise the rose itself in Glasses . . .
> To stew th'Elixir in a bath
> Of Hope, Credulity, and Faith.

Apparently what irritated him, at least in part, was that they
tried "Nature to suborn," and it was common knowledge at
the time that nature was too complex, inexhaustible, and se-
cretive to allow systematic study of the kind proposed.[1]

At the beginning of the nineteenth century, a number of
distinguished critics, philosophers, and poets struggled with
the problem, each with a somewhat different solution. Shelley's *In Defense of Poetry* was a response to a strongly deroga-
tory statement by Thomas Peacock in which he referred to
"the drivelers and mountebanks" who "are contending for
the poetical palm and the critical chair."[2] Shelley's mode of
response was merely to assert, in poetic language, the symbolic,
metaphorical, and inspirational values of poetry; he does not
attack science. Blake's mysticism, as one might expect, leads
him totally away from science, as a thing to be dreaded. From
such a standpoint, I suppose, it makes sense to say that "to

1. See Dorothy Stimson, *Scientists and Amateurs, A History of the Royal
Society* (New York, Abelard-Schumann, 1948), pp. 70–115.

2. Quoted in William Wimsatt and Cleanth Brooks, *Literary Criticism, A
Short History*, p. 417.

generalize is to be an idiot." Coleridge deals with science quite differently. His famous dictum that the purpose of poetry was pleasure and not truth permits him to relax in the presence of science, and in the *Biographia* we find him quite conversant with Hartley and Priestly, dealing with them on equal terms.[3] Arnold solves the problem by assigning to poetry the functions previously performed by philosophy and religion, that is, the interpretation of life. He notes that this interpretation will be required no matter what science finds out about the nature of the world around us. Poetry will answer the question: What will we do with it? and the more science finds out the more the poetic answers will be needed.[4]

Today, with the behavioral sciences as well as the natural sciences making greater claims than ever before, the humanities, seeking to protect "the human values" that they cherish, search for the most effective strategies of defense. Should they assert again the chasm between science and the humanities and withdraw behind it? Should they sally forth to challenge and attack the scientists and particularly those late humanists, the behavioral scientists, who defected in this generation from their parental home? Should they employ the tactics and weapons of the scientists, indeed, embrace them? There are some who do each. Were the problem not couched in terms of defense, they might do none of them: they might peacefully review the instruments of learning and research and select among them those appropriate for an assault, not upon science, but upon the knotty problems of history, philosophy, literature, and art. And there are some who do that, too.

The champions of the chasm agree with John Crowe Ransom: "The critic will doubtless work empirically, and set up his philosophy only as the drift of his findings will compel him. . . . He cannot follow the poets and still conceive himself as inhabiting the rational or 'tidy' universe that is supposed

3. *Complete Works* (New York, 1884) 3, 225–39.
4. "Literature and Science" in *Four Essays on Life and Letters,* ed. E. K. Brown (New York, F. S. Crofts, 1947), pp. 109–10.

by the scientists."[5] Or, taking the view that there are many kinds of truth, he may claim along with the Baroque authors, "Some kinds of truth have to be stated by negation or calculated distortion,"[6] thus burning the bridge of language over the chasm. Or he may retire into ineffable and incommunicable mystery.

If they choose a bolder course and advance to the attack, they may pit wisdom against science: "Not a little of Johnson's wisdom, which exceeded that of most of our phychologists and sociologists of today, came from great literature."[7]

Or they may choose ridicule:

> Thou shalt not sit with statisticians
> Or commit a social science.
> > (W. H. Auden)

Or sarcasm:

> In his extra-laboratory pronouncements the merged philosopher-scientist sounds uncomfortably like his famous creation in allegorical fiction, the 'man in the street'—the man without specialisms who used to sit on the cracker barrel, and who, in all ages since hats were invented, has talked through his hat.[8]

Or defamation:

> The humanist's image (or as we prefer to say, "myth") of the contemporary sociologist is that of a heavily subsidized, much-touted and honored scholar, torn at each moment between offers from industry and government— scarcely knowing, indeed, whether to take the rewards

5. "Criticism as Pure Speculation," in Stauffer, ed., *The Intent of the Critic*, p. 124.

6. See René Wellek and Austin Warren, *Theory of Literature*, p. 187.

7. Norman Foerster, "The Aesthetic Judgment and the Ethical Judgment," in Stauffer, ed., *The Intent of the Critic*, p. 74.

8. Allen Tate, *The Man of Letters in the Modern World*, p. 29.

offered by the Coca-Cola Company or the Air Force—for
his latest documentation of some weary cliché about man,
long since a commonplace of literature.[9]

These attacks reflect a wounded spirit, an anguish no less real
because it has selected the wrong target.

But there is a third mode of dealing with the failure of
knowledge to maintain its historic unity and that is a failure
to perceive real differences, a search for some quick substitute
for the hard and difficult process of theory construction, gath-
ering evidence, testing, and reformulation. Reacting against
"the strong emotional repugnance felt by many critics toward
any form of schematization in poetics," Northrop Frye seeks
to go immediately to the heart of science and to find in mathematics a key to understanding of literature.[10] This is too much,
too soon. One must start where Newton, Boyle, Farraday started—systematic observation and experiment. Finally, as is so
often the case, in our weariness we come to I. A. Richards for
refreshment. Finding the science that most concerned him to
be deficient, he argues "the only possible course is to hasten,
so far as we can, the development of a psychology which ignores none of the facts and yet demolishes none of the values
that human experience has shown to be necessary."[11] Like
Coleridge, at an earlier period, not being afraid of science, he
comes to terms with it.

But, in the meantime, the unity of knowledge lies factured
on the floor. There are at least four disciplines concerned with
the study of language; one of them, the study of literature,
tends to ignore the others.[12] The study of the social source

9. Leslie A. Fiedler, "Voting and Voting Studies," in Eugene Burdick and
Arthur J. Brodbeck, *American Voting Behavior* (Glencoe, Ill., The Free Press,
1959), p. 186.

10. *Anatomy of Criticism*, pp. 35–54.

11. *Practical Criticism*, p. 323.

12. But see Harold B. Allen, ed., *Readings in Applied English Linguistics*
(New York, Appleton-Century-Crofts, 1958). I am indebted to Erwin R. Stein-
berg for drawing my attention to this work.

and function of literature and its authors is abstracted under "Sociology of Language, Literature & Art" in the *Sociology Abstracts;* the study of the way in which literature communicates to the reader and the creative process is abstracted under "Aesthetics" in the *Psychological Abstracts*. But in the recent issues of *PMLA* I find no references to this literature. The sociologists are doing work, for example, on "Political and Social Themes in the English Popular Novel, 1815–1932," on racial themes in literature, on poetry and creativity. The psychologists abstract pieces on "Richard (II) and his Shadow World," "Some Observations on the Symbolism of the Broken Pot in Art and Literature," "Emotion and Feeling in Psychology and Art" (probably a reference to T. S. Eliot's distinction), "Art and Communication," "Goethe's Werther," "One Day I'll Live in the Castle! Cinderella as a Case History." In a roundup of "American Journals in the Humanities" the September 1957 *PMLA* lists forty-eight learned journals dealing with language and literature, but there seems to be hardly any overlap between this world and the world abstracted by the sociologists and psychologists. Of course what the other disciplines do is not criticism, but it would be easy to show the way their work bears on statements made in criticism. The differences in subject matter are real, but partial; it is the methodological, the conceptual, the epistemological differences, however, which make the gulf virtually unbridgeable, and the persistence of these differences is, at the core, based on illusion. The chasm endures and the prophets of division have managed to discover that most effective instrument of all—the self-fulfilling prophecy.

If these observations are correct, it follows that our educational system, partly because it is the guardian of knowledge and the repository of civilization, and partly because it is the tutor to the young, must set about correcting the situation as rapidly as possible. There must be an understanding of the problem and then remedial action.

First, no discipline can afford to exempt itself from the con-

stant effort to formulate and systematize the theoretical presuppositions on which its classifications, typologies, "approaches," "interpretations," even hunches and intuitions, rest.
No discipline can afford, either, to permit these endeavors to
become excessively private, individual, atomized, and heavily
larded with references and terms understood only by the theorist who developed them. I have argued and would defend, too,
the idea that in order to serve one of the most important functions of theory, theoretical statements must be stated in such
a way that their propositions can be used, by subsumption, to
explain or partially explain particular cases. This means that
it must not be merely classificatory; it must have causal components.

In the second place every discipline must work toward a
univocal language; if this involves the invention of terms, the
hyphenation of terms, the appropriation of general terms for
specific well-understood special meanings, let us mourn pri-
vately about this. It is a casualty of a larger good—the communication of knowledge. But, I think, this does not mean
that one must write badly all the time.

There is nothing in our scheme which demotes the analysis
of values, the development of moral clarity, the search for
the ends and purposes and meanings of life. Hence, third,
these must be preserved. But, in the fourth place, every discipline must clarify its procedures so that the comparison,
analysis, and postulation of values is divorced from the evaluation of specific instances, must employ some form of "due
process" in these evaluation procedures, and must keep these,
in turn, separate from the functional analysis of the various
relationships with which the discipline deals. The behavioral
sciences, like the humanities, are not value-free; but they are,
or try to be, value-clear. And, in the true spirit of humanism,
all disciplines should be value-fair; that is, they should proceed
judicially in making judgements.

Fifth, every discipline must look at parts and wholes; if
analysis is reductionist in some sense, there must be a holistic

and reconstitutive portion that redresses the balance. There is an enormous nonsense about the reductionism of the behavioral sciences; but while I reject much of it, I know what is meant. Robert Redfield expresses it in the following terms:

> It is the fact that it is the nature of humanity . . . to cease to be itself in so far as it is decomposed into parts or element. . . . The effort of the scientific mind to reduce the reality to elements amenable to analysis, comparison, and even mensuration early results in a distortion or in the disappearance of the subject matter as common sense knows it.[13]

I have asked behavioral scientists about men and they have told me about variables. That is not what I asked. But, still, Redfield and I understand behavior better because someone has "decomposed" the whole and analyzed the variables. If those who fear the reductionism of analysis imply that one should not penetrate vague concepts with precise instruments, one should not look at the morally sanctified portions of culture with a secular and skeptical mind, one should avoid taking apart some whole, perhaps a myth, a mood, a poem, or a man, to see how he or it is put together, then the work of scholarship stops dead and curiosity becomes an anachronism.

When the Royal Society was in its first decade, some of the subjects which came under the scrutiny of the members of the society elicited great scorn among the learned of the time. Robert Hooke, for example, Boyle's assistant and the author of *Micrographia,* devoted great pains to the analysis of insects and engaged Sir Christopher Wren, also a member of the Society, to make detailed drawings of "a louse, a flea, and a nit."[14] This, of course, was trivial beyond measure, reductionist, and, moreover, probably against the will of God.

---

13. "Relations of Anthropology to the Social Sciences and to the Humanities," in A. L. Kroeber, *Anthropology Today* (University of Chicago Press, 1953), p. 732.

14. Dorothy Stimson, *Scientists and Amateurs*, pp. 76–77.

On the occasion of the dedication of the Sheldonian auditorium at Oxford, Dr. South, the University Orator, declared of these early scientists "They can admire nothing except fleas, lice, and themselves," and he went on to damn what was called "comprehension and the new philosophy."[15] At another time, the ridiculous obsession with instruments and measurement caused King Charles to be greatly amused. As Pepys reported on February 1, 1663/4, the King "mightily laughed at Gresham College for spending time only in weighing of ayre and nothing else."[16]

One of the casualties of the bifurcation of knowledge is the understanding of man. Of course everyone claims him; in a sense he is all we have. Allen Tate remarks that it is the man of letters who must "recreate for his age the image of man, and he must propagate standards by which other men may test that image, and distinguish the false from the true."[17] J. Douglas Bush, the Gurney Professor of English Literature at Harvard, conceives it to be the mission of the humanities to save mankind on the grounds that by studying them "one is never allowed to forget the individual person, to lose sight of one's self and others in a large blur of social and economic forces and formulas."[18] It comes to me as something of a shock and a matter of great regret that, to the extent that there is a "plain sense" meaning in these phrases, precisely the reverse is true—at least this is the case with the critical literature. For the fact of the case is that, except when dealing with biography, critical literature treats large aggregations of undifferentiated human collectives, usually under the categories of "the reader," "the poet," "the artist," or the greatest collectivity of all, "man." One searches almost in vain for something closer to the individual that is not quite biography: certain

15. Quoted in Stimson, p. 77.
16. Quoted in Stimson, p. 80.
17. *The Man of Letters in the Modern World*, p. 11.
18. "The Real Maladjustment," in the Harvard Foundation for Advanced Study and Research *Newsletter*, September 30, 1959.

kinds of poets doing certain kinds of things under certain kinds of conditions; certain kinds of readers enjoying certain effects produced by certain qualities of a poem.

The conclusion, unfortunately, must be that in their concern for words and "a close reading of the poem" some humanists have forgotten about human nature and its wide and interesting variety. Those who are studying man, individually and in his various postures of behavior, are, of course, the behavioral scientists. But do they make their studies lovingly? Do they treat man tenderly? Are they interested in "purposes" as well as "functions"? Do they face squarely the question: "Why are we here?" Lovingly? Perhaps—it is a fact that social scientists are generally more concerned with and about the real sufferings of the underprivileged than humanists.[19] Tenderly? Perhaps not; they must dissect and this is considered untender by some. Purposes? Individually, yes. They deal with men's intentions as well as their actions. But for all mankind, as in the question on the purpose of life, no, they do not. Hence they do not seek answers to the question "Why are we here?" But they know how real people all over the world answer this question, and that is something. This is simply saying that the behavioral scientist knows about human beings, although he does not know the Divine Will. But it is human behavior, not Divine Behavior which is his specialty.

The opening up of communication between the humanities and the social sciences, and the development of common languages and methods, wherever appropriate, will not, then, face one "image of man" with another. But it will do something else. Mythology has lent its names to psychoanalysis (Oedipus, Narcissus, Eros, Thanatos) for a very good reason. Characters in fiction, like Micawber and Oblomov, focus attention upon styles of behavior and attitudinal types. I have seen courses in public administration starting with Trollope, *The Three Clerks,* and have heard it argued that the best way to approach

19. See Chapter 8, footnote 9.

the study of Soviet politics is through nineteenth- and twen-
tieth-century Russian novels. There is some congruence between national character and national literature; the study of
culture as a social product leads to the study of literature and
art. In short, the humanities stimulate the behavioral sciences,
give "inspired" subjectively screened portraits of men and so-
cieties in motion, and give life and drama to the behavioral
scientists' categories and findings. Max Eastman says they
help us to understand what, through the sciences, in another
sense, we already know.[20] "Understand" means round out, fill
in the details, give motion to static concepts, engage empathic
sentiments, enlist, in short, *verstehen*. But for this purpose,
the behavioral scientist must meet the literary critic half way;
he must join in the analytic, critical process.

What I have been saying may lead some to the conclusion
that a proper method will give proper answers. That is wrong.
The proper questions, plus the proper method, will be more
likely to give proper answers. Any method may be abused, as
Aristotle noted in his *Rhetoric* when he cautioned that the
Sophists might abuse certain verbal tricks and methods. Any
method can give sterile answers if the questions asked are not
fruitful, and the substance of literature, as well as its theory,
can help to pose fruitful questions.

An alternative and equally wrong conclusion that might
be drawn from these remarks would be to the effect that some
separate course of instruction—a course in logic, say, or in
scientific methods isolated from the substantive matter to be
taught—could solve the problem. There might be voices
raised in behalf of this suggestion, for it would permit men to
go on thinking and teaching in their accustomed ways, happy
to have their consciences cleared with so little effort on their
part. Such courses should, of course, be central to the curricu-
lum—they are as important to the liberal arts as mathematics
is to the sciences. Yet, although it is true that one of the foun-

20. *The Literary Mind: Its Place in an Age of Science.*

dation stones of my entire argument is that the ways of thinking encouraged in one area of learning tend to be applied in another, I must nevertheless maintain that the teaching of logic and the scientific method isolated from the subject matter of learning, empty of poetry and politics alike, promises only a little improvement. Unless it is wedded to the materials for which it is a guide, unless it is *used* over and over again, unless the teachers of the subject themselves employ a clarity of mind such as we have spoken for, the learning in methods will be the Sunday morality of the weekday sinner. One of the most forceful teachings of psychoanalysis is that insight is not enough; one must "work through" the new learning to make it useful.

The lowly scope and methods courses of the behavioral sciences, humble and abused as they are, offer some slender thread of hope. The thread is slender because we have had enough experience with the methods courses of the teachers colleges to have earned a massive skepticism about this vehicle of learning. To the extent that they focus upon how to use a library, how to collect a bibliography, how to interview, how to build a maze for rats, how to scan a poem, and so forth, they belong to the janitorial services of learning—indispensable, but janitorial. But for those moments when they deal with the problem of how to think about the structure of knowledge in their discipline, how to infer from evidence, how to construct a theory—and how to test it, how and when to generalize and how to limit generalization—all in close connection with a substantive body of material, and all dirtied by data—those moments, I believe, are fruitful for a discipline and pregnant with possibilities for the advancement of understanding.

But they are only moments, and, as Dewey remarks, experience is continuous. There is no other solution than the continuous re-examination of the objective foundations of our concepts, theories, and beliefs in a hard-headed and scientific way by all concerned with learning. Imagination and feeling are tender growths; do not damage them. But all the same and

all the time for all of us there must be that grinding molecular
process milling out the answers to the questions how do we
know? how good is the evidence? how far can we generalize?
what are the theoretical premises? what is the definition? how
is this information structured, classified, organized? The human values of the humanities speak to our emotions; that is
where love is located. But civilization rests also upon the mind,
the hard cruel mind, the desiccating, withering analytical
mind. And this is not memory—that is what a library is for
—but analysis.

What I am talking about here is a kind of self-conscious
attention to the organization of thought and evidence, values
and experience within the context of a subject matter. No
trivial part of the usefulness of such organization is the sorting
out of the various kinds of mental functioning discussed
above; the autistic and the directed thought processes, the
immediate and mediated perception, the referential and non-
referential expression, the employment of analyzed and un-
analyzed concepts. These distinctions are crucial to the entire
thinking operation. Richards says of the distinction between
making a referential statement and the encitement of an attitude:

> There is hardly a problem outside mathematics which is
> not complicated by its neglect, and hardly any emotional
> response which is not crippled by its irrelevant intrusions.
> No revolution in human affairs would be greater than
> that which a widespread observance of this distinction
> would bring about.[21]

And this is true of all of them. Suddenly—or rather gradually
—we would find that we were communicating with each other,
often for the first time.

The emphasis upon the organization of thought and the
verification of knowledge is often unwanted because it seems

21. *Principles of Literary Criticism*, p. 274.

to challenge two specialists: the man of sensibility and the man of information. The man of sensibility who can himself discriminate and make refined judgments, who claims and often has something that is loosely called intuition, but who cannot systematize his skill or state the principles according to which he operates, inevitably feels threatened, even degraded by the efforts of others to analyze the very processes of sensibility. To the extent that he opposes the effort, he is indeed challenged—and he will be overwhelmed by the glacial advances of science. To the extent that he continues to do what *he* can do best, better than anybody else, he maintains standards of performance for the systematizers to emulate, and to explain.

The man of information feels threatened because his strength lies in his memory drum, which, like a computer, can recall an infinite assortment of relevant data when asked the right question. But information alone does not lead to understanding. The confusion of information and thought is a central problem for historians whose discipline tends to stress information, because, in a sense, history is social memory, but it also arises in the discussions of the arts and the social sciences. The critic who is best informed on the allusions of a work of art is not, by that reason alone, best able to explain how it achieves its effects or to interpret its power to communicate. In order to do this, he must raise to the conscious level the theoretical premises he employs, clarify his concepts and classification schemes, have a sense of what is verifiable and verified, and draw logical deductions about any present instance.

But the strengths of the man of information are no less important to the processes we have in mind; this is not a counsel of ignorance. So many dialogues come to mind of the following nature: the theorist says "Modern civilization tends to make men live longer." The man of information answers "Methuselah." The theorist re-examines his theory and it appears that the life expectancy of those over eighty years old has remained constant for 3,000 years; a modification of his theory, and an interesting point to pursue further, and incidentally, probably true.

By now it must be clear that the diversity of scholarly needs, combined with the wide range of skills and interests, makes a happy situation where the division of labor is a felicitous principle. The systematizer—and there must be one and he must know his business—the model builder, the middle-gauge theorist, the intuitive interpreter, the historical scholar, the experimentalist, the methodologist, the inter-disciplinary explorer or emigré, are all required. A discipline that neglects any of them does so at its peril, impoverishes itself, invites anemia, and begs for invasion. But the lush variety of specialisms and generalisms suggested must be endogenous, or partly so. The stranger is seen as an invader and men gather together and forget their own differences to resist invasion. Yet I must believe that this stranger in the present case has a stake in all learning processes, for he is a citizen, not of a far country, but of the same nation, and a peripatetic neighbor in the same sacred grove.

Index

Date Due